Mastaclass Magic
True Journey to Health, Happiness, Love, Success

PRIDE AND PREJUDICE PREVAIL
The First Memoir

Peter Muir

i

Library of Congress Cataloging in Publication Data

ISBN: 978 9769578708

ISBN:

PRAISE for "PRIDE AND PREJUDICE PREVAIL"

"GREAT!!!!
I read it nonstop! I have the impression that I have
not only read but seen it! I love your detailed
report of your childhood and youth from
downtown Kingston to Harvard".

Ulla Leis

"Peter Muir's memoirs relate, with refreshing
honesty and candor, tales of personal growth,
struggle and determination to triumph over
tremendous obstacles. As I read the manuscript I
realized how valuable it would be for young
persons, an inspirational gem to empower them to
meet their own challenges with confidence and
courage."

Allison Holness McGraham

To my mother, Edna Vivienne Muir (nee Aaron) for instilling in me the thirst for knowledge, the caring for neighbor and the passion for truth and justice.

To my beloved wife, Beverley, nee Hanson, without whose insistence that I should write my autobiography, my memoirs may have not been written.

Acknowledgements

To my cousin Jackie Stuart who provided advice, childhood stories, the Journey and other images for the book, and also to his family for their example of family unity and love.

To Catholic nun Sister Philomena, headmistress of Holy Family Elementary School and Catholic priest Father McMullan, headmaster of St. George's College, a Jamaican High School. They provided guidance and created a path to my High School and University education.

To David Ludtke, my room-mate at Harvard University and best friend, who made my college experience so much more enjoyable. No words can express my appreciation for his wonderful caring and support, with which I continue to be blessed.

To Allison Holness McGraham who encouraged me to complete the writing of my memoirs, describing an early draft as "an inspirational gem that could inspire youngsters to achieve their dreams against seemingly insurmountable odds."

To Kadija George, editor, author, publisher, who provided free writing advice and encouragement

To Meleisa Witter for dedicated editing of *Pride and Prejudice Prevail*, my first memoir.

Disclaimer

To create a story --- and because memory is sometimes unreliable, interpretations and perspectives vary, and access to detailed knowledge of some incidents is limited --- creative license has been taken in describing some people and places and relating details of events and conversations. Names of some people and places have been changed, but some characters are named, or may be recognizable as known persons. [Note that all fictitious names of actual persons are starred (*).]

The story is told from diverse observations and fragmented and sometimes unreliable memories, including memories of individuals whose perspective was shaped by trauma and years of suffering, pain, struggle and cruel injustices. There is no intention to defame or criticize individuals about whose life, other deeds, endeavors and deeper motives and intentions neither the author nor the protagonist has knowledge. Rather, the goal is to expose how their thinking and conduct in specific situations was influenced by a flawed system and the social prejudices of the day; and how it was perceived by, reacted to and affected the victims of society's failure.

The criticism of those who continue, today, to support injustice, to misrepresent history, and to discriminate based on sex, race, class, wealth, education and/or religion is, however, deliberate and made without apology.

In this vein, this book is unapologetically for *all* wonderful individuals, 13 years and over, regardless of gender, class or creed.

Contents

Foreword

The first Memoir "Pride and Prejudice Prevail" of Peter Muir's series, *Mastaclass Magic*, tells the amazing story of his childhood experiences. Despite placing first at elementary school in every class every year and reaching high school age in 1949, Peter could not attend high school for three years due to financial constraints. No government high schools were yet built and my poor family was unable to pay for private education. From age eleven years he worked after school and during holidays to earn his high school fees, and entered St. George's three years later in 1952. Yet he achieved the highest Jamaican grades in the 1955 British Senior Cambridge Examinations and was valedictorian of his high school graduating class. Taking the U.S. SAT examinations, he ranked in the 97th percentile (top 3%) of participants in the world. He won several scholarships, including a full international scholarship to Harvard University, without prior knowledge of its prestige and Number 1 academic ranking in the world.

In 1961 he returned to Jamaica immediately after graduating with the Bachelor of Arts degree majoring in Chemistry and worked with multinational corporations in Kingston. He has given dedicated service to many charitable and community organizations. He also founded a scholarship program in his Rotary Club to assist inner-city youths in Kingston. He was awarded "Volunteer of the Year 2006" for dedicated commitment to community and nation building in association with the United Nations Volunteer Program.

It is imperative that we get to a place within our consciousness where we come to the deep realization that we were born with ability, creativity, and spirituality, to love and be loved, to respect and be respected, to have great relationships, to attract our soul-mates, to be healthy, happy and successful. If at this point that is not an accurate description of your life, then I am not just being kind when I say "It is not your fault, not entirely. The good news is that it is not too late to turn your life around and get on the path to your true destiny, to be MASTACLASS."

There are tremendous benefits to be gained by reading this book. You will be inspired to:
- Overcome adversity to be your best self
- Achieve your goals, hopes and dreams
- Serve your God in spirit and in truth

Prologue

What if magic could help you to achieve good health, lasting happiness, true love and personal success? What if you have all the MAGIC you need lying dormant inside you that just need to be awakened? It is for this very reason why this book has been written. MASTACLASS denotes mastery of your thoughts, emotions, speech, actions and habits; identifying with all the classes; accepting the good and rejecting the bad values and attitudes of each class. MASTACLASS does not require having, nor does it exclude a lot of money and power. In my series of memoirs you will read stories from which the concept of MASTACLASS was born. Stories which tell of my struggles to overcome bad parenting, poverty, unhappiness, ill health, corrupt religious dogma and scarce opportunities for quality education, to achieve the ultimate goal of human beings; self-love, self-esteem, self-fulfillment, financial security and personal success.

My book, *MASTACLASS MAGIC: True Journey to Health, Happiness, Love and Success*, is intended to inspire primarily teenagers and young adults to discover their true nature and essential needs in order to achieve self-love, self-esteem, close relationships, a beloved and loving soul mate, lasting happiness and personal success. Older persons will benefit too, and become more aware of the need to assist their children, younger relatives and friends to be healthy, caring, happy, successful, and responsible citizens. Ultimately, my desire is to leave MASTACLASS as a lasting legacy which can be recognized as my contribution to the world in a bid to make it a better place for all people.

My life's journey is an extra-ordinary story of transformation that started with my awareness in childhood of the inequality, prejudice, discrimination and injustice that prevailed in my family, my community and my country Jamaica. However, Catholic Sunday School taught me that the Son of God, Jesus of Nazareth, preached love of neighbor, non-discrimination and justice for all. Because my mother, Edna Aaron, was darker than my father's fair-skinned mother, Mrs. Laura Ward, called Gangang by her grandchildren, she was implacably opposed to the marriage of Edna to her son, who could pass for white, and treated Mama as a servant she disliked.

Only recently in my seventies did I fully realize that my early childhood experiences were a transformational period that fashioned me into the unhappy, teenage rebel I became. Rejecting many of the society's values, attitudes and actions considered unjust and discriminatory, I embraced the religious teaching of Jesus' ministry. This profoundly influenced my behavior with good and bad consequences for my entire life. Perhaps subconsciously, I compared the doctrines, beliefs and behavior of family, society and institutions against the ministry and life story of Jesus, and found many of them wanting. Consequently, I developed a distrust and lack of respect for persons of authority. I boldly disobeyed some instructions of parents, teachers, priests, and later bosses, which I considered unethical, discriminatory, unfair or unjust. I was on a path determined to do the right thing by following Jesus' ministry on my journey throughout my life.

Somehow, sometime during my early childhood, consciously and/or subconsciously, I started to reject the extreme classism and prejudice of Jamaican society. I took the first steps on my journey to become what I term, MASTACLASS, not identifying myself as belonging to any one of royalty, upper-class, middleclass, or lower-class. Throughout his life, Jesus manifested these characteristics, which are rarely practiced by the majority of 'Christians.' I became able to think independently of society's values and religious dogma. I could identify with the positive features of, and be comfortable among, any and all of the classes. However, it was not until further transformation throughout my later adult years that I fully realized that my knee-jerk, confrontational response to what I perceived as untrue, discriminatory and/or unjust, was not in the best interest of my God, my neighbor or myself. We would all have been better served if I had been able to state my convictions in a bold, but friendly, respectful and charming manner, designed to win friends and influence people.

Fortunately, I heeded my mother's advice that my best chance for a better, successful life was a good education; a goal to which she dedicated herself to achieve for all her children. I paid keen attention at the unregistered zinc-shed infant school I attended in a nearby yard on Tower Street. In this first memoir, I describe my struggles against living a typical Jamaican discriminatory lifestyle while striving to achieve a better life by excelling at my schoolwork. In our rapidly changing world, so advanced in knowledge, education, science and technology, health, travel, communication, and entertainment, children today will have a different experience from my childhood days. Nevertheless, age-old traditions concerning beliefs, governance, religion, values and behavior are being challenged now more than ever. The need to challenge oneself to live a more aware, engaged, healthy, happy and successful life is perhaps greater now than ever before. Despite the improvements in health, homes, education, technology, travel, communication and entertainment, people of all classes are dissatisfied with so many aspects of their lives– relationships, shelter, health, sex, money; resulting in unhappiness, boredom, depression and frustration. Many persons feel a deep desire for something more than health, money, possessions, partners, and career success. If I may use my experience as a judge, they are probably faced with the need to achieve self-love, self-respect, close relationships, lasting happiness and personal success.

I have achieved happiness and the fulfillment of all my personal desires. I keep on reading and learning new ideas and valuable information for life improvement. I consciously decided during my life's journey to transform myself in various ways, always striving to be a better person. I never gave up until in my seventies all my personal hopes and dreams were finally achieved. My mission now is to help as many persons as I can to achieve their true happiness and personal fulfillment. I believe that everyone can achieve more self-love, self-respect, close relationships, lasting happiness and personal success through caring for others, setting goals, ongoing learning, hard work and determination, seeking help and never giving up. Yes, you can.

This first memoir relates some of my childhood experiences and the profound effect they had on my emotions, my thoughts, my speech, my actions, my relationships, my passions and my goals, which formed my initial childhood philosophy for living. It describes the foundation that I, with the timely help and encouragement in my childhood of a few "guardian angels" would build on to eventually achieve MASTACLASS. You may also choose to read the second memoir, *"Lifelong Learning, Your Sure Path to Good Health and Financial Success"*, the third *"Love, Lust or Lunacy"* and the fourth, *"Beware Expert Opinion"* before you will begin to acquire all the necessary knowledge, thoughts, actions and habits to achieve the benefits to be derived from the entire book of memoirs.

IF by Rudyard Kipling (Excerpt)

If you can keep your head when all about you
Are losing theirs and blaming it on you,
If you can trust yourself when all men doubt you,
But make allowance for their doubting too;
If all men count with you, but none too much;
Or walk with Kings---nor lose the common touch,
Yours is the Earth and everything that's in it,
And---which is more---you'll be a Man, my son!

Rudyard Kipling, the prolific author and composer of the poem "If" visited Jamaica in February 1930. I, Peter Oliver Muir, have been inspired to live the life the poem describes. I have kept my faith in the ministry of Jesus. I will try to illustrate my interpretation of Jesus' ministry in a few words and phrases as follows:

Worship your 'God,' love yourself, your family and your friends, care for your neighbor (everyone you encounter). In thought, speech, actions and habits, strive for the greater good of all mankind, not only for your personal benefit. Practice justice, non-discrimination, honesty, fair play, caring, forgiveness, and compassion. Be thankful for your blessings. Work hard to achieve your goals. Share your assets and your knowledge with those in need. In summary, try to be the best that you can be.

From childhood, I rejected the unjust doctrines and behavior of my family, of my friends, of my society and the unjust laws of my country and the world. I have loved, and been loved, truly and passionately. I am enjoying peace and happiness that lasts, no matter what. I have achieved personal success, personal fulfillment, all my dreams, and more. My marriage to Beverley lasted more than forty loving years. I had a very close and joyful paternal relationship with my two children, Susan and David. I believe that I have been transformed and evolved from being the son of my father into being a 'Man.' My son David has told me that I inspired him to care deeply and love truly to achieve his own happiness and personal success.

Here is my message to people who want to live the best life of which they are capable:

Young man, young woman, you too can have good health, true love, lasting happiness and personal success. Yes you can. Believe in yourself. Be passionate and determined to achieve your dreams. Keep on caring, learning, work hard and smart, seek help and never give up. I sincerely hope that my memoirs will inspire you to be the best that you can be; and ultimately achieve all your personal goals and dreams, as I did.

My older friends, it is not too late to achieve a life with better health, passionate love, lasting happiness and personal success. Parents, care for, encourage and support your children to achieve their hopes and dreams, not yours.

CHAPTER ONE

Seeking my Ancestors

I conjecture a scene which may have happened in the late 1920s.

"Edna," my father Richmond Alexander Muir declared passionately, "I will marry you with or without my mother's approval. I love you. Nothing and nobody can keep us apart!"

"Your mother will never accept me as your wife," Edna replied glumly, her beauty unmarred by the downcast expression etched so painfully across her usually vivacious, lively face. "She was so disappointed and angry when you told her that we were engaged. She was emphatic that she would never allow her son to marry a black girl."

"I am an adult and I don't need her permission; I can marry whomever I please. You are the only one for me Edna." Richmond declared, sounding unusually defiant.

"Richmond, I don't want to cause any discord between you and your mother. She will surely not allow me to live in her house, nor would I feel comfortable there." Edna replied, trying to reason with him, though it broke her heart and made her feel like crying.

"I will talk to her," Richmond assured his fiancé. "Perhaps she has calmed down and will now be more reasonable." At least he hoped that was the case. After all, his mind had already been made up this time.

The intensely passionate exchange took place in the cafeteria at Times Store; Edna's workplace on King Street in Kingston, the capital city of the island of Jamaica. Richmond was a handsome young man. He was 29 years of age, and of a very light complexion with European features. His least compelling physical attribute was his height. Considered short for a male, he stood at five feet 6 inches tall. Edna was 22 years old, and a few inches shorter than Richmond at 5 feet 4 inches. She had light-brown skin and sparkling grey eyes in a pretty, almost round face. Richmond Alexander Muir, my father, was fair skinned enough to pass for 'white' anywhere. I assume that he was the illegitimate son of a 'white' Scotsman. I have not been told or been able to learn, despite great efforts, anything about my paternal grandfather. Mrs. Laura Ward, or Gangang, as we called our fair-skinned, mulatto grandmother, insisted my father should not marry the 'black girl' he loved.

Edna was a little darker than my grandmother, neither of whom could pass for white. Try as he might, Gangang remained inalterably opposed to the marriage. Although he did not want to offend his mother, Richmond was determined to marry Edna. "Could they find a way to make their marriage work without his mother's help and support?" he wondered. He was working as a typesetter for the Jamaica Mail newspaper. Edna was employed as a sales clerk at Times Store on King Street. Fortunately, they both had some money saved. They started seeking a suitable, affordable house to rent. After several weeks without success, Edna suggested an alternative plan for their marital home.

"Richmond, you know that my cousin Edmund Foster builds homes. I have already spoken to him and he is willing to help us. Do you think that we could pool our savings to buy a piece of land and get a mortgage loan to build a small house?"

"That is an excellent idea" Richmond enthused, "I will contact Victoria Mutual Building Society to determine their requirements for the loan."

On one of the rare occasions he ever did, Papa defied his mother. On the fourth of March 1930, he married Edna Vivienne Aaron, in Holy Trinity Cathedral. The witnesses were Amos M. Browne and Eva Street. They moved into modest rented premises until they had pooled enough savings in 1932 to buy a plot of land on Oliver Road. Victoria Mutual Building Society provided the mortgage loan to finance building the house on the land. Papa also later inherited a car from his grandmother who was fairly wealthy. He never learned how to drive however and so never benefitted from his inheritance. But the house did not remain a family property for long and the children neither grew up in it nor inherited it.

Shortly after the house was built, things took a turn for the worse with Richmond and Edna.

A few months before he died at the ripe old age of 102, a reporter from the Gleaner Company interviewed Papa. In the article published in the Star daily newspaper, Papa related what happened to his house and car.

"Soon after I moved into the house, the company I worked with, The Jamaica Mail, closed down and I was out of a job." It was during this period that he said he made the biggest mistake of his life. Desperation forced his hand and he made a decision and took some actions that he would never recover from as long as he lived. "I could not pay the bank for the loan, so I sold the house for 300 British pounds when it was valued at over 1000 pounds." He explained, "You see, money had to be going out but none was coming in." He also revealed another shortcoming which contributed to the later hardships faced by his family as he lost another asset through a lack of concern.

When he was moving out of his house, Papa related that he sat around the steering wheel of his car, but did not drive it. The reporter asked, "So what was wrong with the car?"

"Well... nothing, but I never learned to drive so I made my cousin Joe tow it with his car all the way to my mother's home."

"What became of your car?"

He responded, "I want to know myself. Well, I never moved my car. As far as I know, I left the car the same place there, but until now, I don't know where it went."

After being forced to sell their home, in 1934 my parents moved into a one-bedroom apartment upstairs Gangang's premises at her house on Highholborn Street. The two-story building occupied most of the small land area. Downstairs was constructed with brick walls and upstairs made entirely of wood with zinc roofing. There were no bathrooms, piped water or electricity services inside the building. At night, kerosene tin lamps with glass shades provided light. The gate opened to a narrow brick walkway. To the immediate right was the single external toilet for the entire household; to the immediate left was the front door of my grandmother's small 'sitting' room, behind which was a guest room. Her bedroom came next, then her dining room, which opened on the right side to a small kitchen area with a gate out to the brick walkway. The kitchen had no facilities other than an icebox and two iron coal stoves on a brick shelf.

The eighteen occupants of the building, comprising two extended families, shared the single zinc enclosed shower. Between the kitchen and the shower was a small open space with a brick shelf, which was used as the 'kitchenette' for my mother. The small, dilapidated structure housing the single toilet with an overhead tank was made entirely of zinc sheets on a wooden frame. Water was available from a standpipe above a cistern in the front yard, another standpipe in the backyard, and the shower. Two outside wooden staircases provided access to the rooms upstairs. The narrow walkway led to a small backyard with an almond tree, a guinep tree and two coconut trees. Midway the length of the walkway was a large ackee tree, scraping against a long, high concrete wall that comprised the entire northern boundary.

My family lived upstairs above my grandmother's premises. My parents and their eight children were cramped in less square footage than my grandmother occupied downstairs. Space and facilities were very limited for a family of two adults and eight children. Our home consisted of a narrow verandah, a bedroom and a living room. At the rear of the living room, a small bedroom was partitioned for my father's use. A wooden staircase that rose westward from the south side of the cistern up to the verandah was used to connect the floors. In my father's small bedroom, the furniture consisted of an iron framed single bed, a bedside table, a wardrobe and a chair. The large bedroom had a wooden dining table with six chairs, a wardrobe, a chest of drawers and one iron framed double bed with a metal spring and a coir mattress. The spring sagged. The mattress cover was torn in so many places that no one lying on the bed could escape the pricking of coir on some parts of his body. To add to the discomfort, the bed was periodically infected with fleas and all efforts to eradicate them met with limited success as soon enough, they returned again. The bed served not only all the children, but Mama as well. She was sometimes welcomed on Papa's single bed for sex and usually returned to the family bedroom before dawn. We couldn't all hold on the one bed. Those who did, were cramped together tighter than sardines in a can. Some occasionally chose to sleep on the floor. I preferred to sleep on the dining table where the fleas mercifully left me alone.

My grandmother's nephew, my uncle Joseph Stewart and his family also lived at 11 Highholborn Street. Their premises consisted of a downstairs living/dining/bed room with a double bed, an upstairs bedroom and a large, open zinc-covered shed used as their kitchen beyond the staircase in the backyard. They were considered poor relations by my grandmother, perhaps even after our family became poorer than theirs.

It was not until my adult years that I learnt that in my grandmother's youth, her family had been fairly well off and could have given claim to being solid middle class citizens. Her mother Josephine Figueroa, affectionately called Mother Jo, traveled and traded goods between Jamaica and Panama. She took Jamaican produce to sell in Panama and returned with Panamanian goods to sell in Jamaica. She was a pioneer higgler (Jamaican term for an unlicensed, individual trader). This is now a popular occupation for many Jamaican women of the middle and lower classes, renamed 'informal commercial trader.' She also profited from her dealings in real estate. The business was successful to the extent that she could eventually afford to buy a dark green Raleigh car and hire a chauffeur. The car was the one papa inherited and later lost through negligence.

My cousin Jackie Stuart with the help of his eldest sister reconstructed the following events regarding Mother Jo's activities. The back yard of Mother Jo's house had a storeroom and a brick oven. Around Christmas time a Garden Party was held at Winchester Park, the sports field at St. George's College, a Catholic High School for boys. Mother Jo would use the oven to bake cakes and cookies; she also made sandwiches and drinks which were sold at the party. All the proceeds from the sale of these refreshments would be donated to the Catholic Church. She had coffins made in various sizes and donated them to poor families when a member died, so that they could have a proper Catholic funeral. The storeroom containing the basic wooden coffins was named 'Lawd-mi-dun' by the neighbors. This space later served as the kitchen for the Stuart family's household.

Sunday was a special day for Granny Jo. As children, we could not play or make any noise, or she would get very upset. She viewed that time as being very sacred and holy and a time to do good works. Granny Jo was kind to the poor families who lived in the community. She had helpers (Jamaican term for household servants) who would go to her house and cook big pots of food and she would invite the people in the community to come and have their luxury dinner. When dinner was over, she had benches placed in front of the house and children from the community would attend Sunday school from 3:00 pm – 4:30 pm. A priest from the Catholic Church would be in charge.

It is very likely that the children attended the Sunday school more for the free food than for the religious instruction. Due to financial constraints, many of the children in the neighborhood did not attend elementary school and would grow up to be illiterate adults. Granny Jo apparently thought that knowledge of religion was more important than secular education, since she is not reported to have helped with the children's schooling. She probably believed that her efforts to promote the work of the church would improve her chances of going to heaven after death, and avoiding the eternal fire of hell.

Granny Jo was a devout Catholic who believed that Jesus Christ was the Son of God and our Savior from sin and hell. Although I admire Granny Jo's religious faith and her philanthropic activities, I think that she was too focused on her Catholic religious teaching. I doubt that she was acting in the best interests of herself, her family, or her neighbors. Perhaps she and all Christians would be better served by greater thought of, and adherence to, the teachings of Christ. He exhorted us to worship God and to love our neighbor as ourselves. He constantly taught by word and by example that we should care for all persons, especially the children. Some of the money Granny Jo gave to the church and spent on its activities may have been more beneficial to her family and neighbors by spending it on education and skills training.

People throughout the world may one day come to realize that they should not place total faith in one particular religious sect and all its teaching. Christians should focus on the teaching and life of Christ, the origin and source of their religion. They should examine and try to follow the teaching and ministry of Christ. They should consider and determine the needs of their neighbors, in order to make informed decisions of how best to serve their neighbors and their God.

As mentioned earlier, Mother Jo had acquired many assets and had left her business in order by way of a will upon her death. However, there is an interesting twist to the story of Mother Jo's will and the effect that the inheritance had upon the family members. She had bequeathed a substantial amount of her assets to the Catholic Church in exchange for prayers for her and her dead husband's souls. Before her passing however, on hearing that he had been left nothing in her will, Uncle Joseph Stewart had protested strongly. She had complied and changed her will to give him a life tenancy; that is, occupancy until his death, of Palm Beach, a property she had bequeathed to the Catholic Church. Palm Beach is a property at Seven Miles in St. Thomas with the Cane River running through it into the Caribbean Sea. Uncle Joe built a shop and bar near the entrance and charged admission to the beach, but these activities afforded him only a modest income throughout my childhood. By virtue of paying the land taxes for many years, Uncle Joe eventually gained ownership and received the title to the property. By selling sand and gravel from the bed of the river running through the property, he eventually became a wealthy man. A small lot of land with no beachfront, adjoining Palm Beach was willed to my father. My sister Laura also acquired ownership of this property by paying the land taxes, built her home on the land and eventually sold it.

After Mother Jo's death, an advertisement appeared in the Daily Gleaner of August 4, 1936 for the sale of three of her properties by public auction. This advertisement was apparently being orchestrated by my grandmother.

FOR SALE BY PUBLIC AUCTION
I am instructed by the Executor
of the Estate of the late Josephine
Figueroa Dowden to sell at my
Auction room on Wednesday, 5th
August 1936 at 11 a.m. the fol-
lowing properties:
NO. 61 MATTHEWS LANE,
12 rooms
NO. 9 ½ HIGHHOLBORN STREET
5 rooms.
NO. 11 ½ HIGHHOLBORN STREET
5 rooms and a small shop.
This is a good opportunity for
investors as the places are all ten-
anted and will give a good income.
CECIL E. BURTON
Auctioneer, Valuator, Real Estate
and Commission Agent.
S/W Corner Water Lane and Duke
Street, Kingston.

In her will, Granny Jo had left a fair sum of money and several properties to my grandmother. But in contrast to Granny Jo who worked hard to earn a good living, Gangang did not engage in any business activities and in fact soon squandered all her inheritance with the help of her 'friends', who handled her business dealings and cheated her. Her only son, my father, was a weakling to whom she entrusted none of her affairs. She disposed of all her inherited property except the family home. By the time of my birth in 1937, my family had become poor. As the neighborhood worsened and her family and former friends moved away, she gradually became estranged from most of them. She snubbed the new neighbors, who were poor and darker colored, and avoided any association with them.

During the 1920s to 1930s, the middle class moved out of downtown Kingston into the suburbs in the parish of St Andrew. Our family home was located at 11 Highholborn Street in Central Kingston, a downtown neighborhood called Southside, inhabited by mostly destitute and very poor families.

Historical Perspective

In 1937, the year of my birth, Jamaica was a British Colony ruled by the Crown Colony form of government in which an English governor was appointed by Britain. The Governor exercised executive and virtually autocratic powers, with advice from a Privy Council consisting entirely of officials and the Governor's nominees. The Legislative Council was comprised of a mix of nominated, ex-officio, and elected members with the required income and property qualifications. Women had even greater restrictions imposed on them, in that, in addition to the preceding requirements, they had to be 25 years old and literate. Thus, the electorate represented about ten percent of the adult population. During the colonial period, the civil service hierarchy reflected the wider West Indian societal pattern. In this rigid stratification of whites, colored, browns and blacks, the latter were confined to clerical positions. They were restricted to assembling papers and passing them up the line to expatriate officials who monopolized the ultimate decision-making positions.

The 1943 Jamaica census found that blacks accounted for eighty per cent of the population, colored (mixed race with fair skin color) fifteen per cent, whites one per cent, Chinese and Chinese-colored one per cent, the Indians and Indian-colored two per cent, and others one per cent. In a paper titled *The Social Structure of Jamaica*, George Cumper analyzed the census tables and commented thus:

> "A fundamental fact is the linkage between poverty and African blood; many of the social distinctions follow from this. African blood was identified with poverty and illiteracy, and that fact, combined with the rigidity of the class structure in a society where opportunities are very unequal, is a principal reason why black skin is still linked with low social standing."

The Jamaican upper and middle classes were tenaciously clinging to what they considered to be the values and attitudes of the mother country, England. Color and class prejudice dominated every sphere of activity and even dark Negroes would feel that they were superior to another of darker skin. Beauty was ascribed only to persons with European features. Kinky (African) hair was popularly described as bad hair. White or very fair-skinned Jamaicans exclusively filled jobs in upscale businesses, shops and banks. The majority of poor, black Jamaicans never married, and the few that did, usually wed after living together for years and having all their children. Therefore, most black Jamaicans bore the stigma of being bastards, for which they were condemned and deemed inferior by upper class society although they were innocent of the 'sin' of unmarried sex that produced them. The bastards begotten by upper class persons were not usually accepted by their families and many were shunned for the rest of their lives, often with little or no financial support. The 'justice system' supported this unjust and discriminatory practice and accorded the bastard children no support or inheritance rights.

There was a noticeable cultural divide between the upper classes in the towns and the black peasants of the rural areas. The white and colored middle classes viewed the black, rural peasants as inferior creatures and called them 'quashie,' a derogatory term implying backward and slow-witted. In his book, *Jamaica*, Oliver Abrahams wrote, "And because he was seen thus, and was sensitive to their attitude to him, he responded with a cold withdrawal that made for two Jamaicas." The Jamaican poet, Claude McKay, caught the mood in the Jamaican dialect:

> *You tase petater an you say it sweet.*
> *But you no know how hard we wuk fe it.*
> *You want a basketful fe quattie.*
> *Cause you nuh know how tiff de bush fe cut.*

> **Possible Translation**
> *You taste potato and say it is sweet.*
> *But you don't realize how hard we work to grow it.*
> *You want to buy a large quantity for a few cents.*
> *You don't know the difficulty to prepare the land.*

The concept of two Jamaicas, which I will label as *'Jamaica up'* and *'Jamaica down'*, was reinforced by the fact that the factions spoke different languages. 'Jamaica up' consisted of a small upper and middle class, the whites and the fair-skinned or 'colored's, whereas 'Jamaica down' comprised the poor, black majority. The well-to-do spoke the 'Queens English,' the quashies spoke patois; a dialect arising from a blend of English and West African tribal languages, which ignored the grammatical rules of standard English.

In Gladstone Mills' book, *'Grist for the Mills,'* he writes, "At the turn of the nineteen thirties, agriculture and agricultural products still formed the bedrock of the Jamaican society. Sugar and bananas were the primary assets, followed by citrus and coffee. Tourism was in its infancy, centered in Port Antonio and Montego Bay, on the basis of the reportedly curative powers of the water of Doctor's Cave beach. Kingston, the capital city of Jamaica, boasted a quintet of famous hotels: Constant Spring, Mona Great House, Manor House, South Camp Road, and Myrtle Bank, none of which exist today. Landed proprietors and managers of the sugar and banana estates, and merchant businessmen of downtown Kingston, dominated the social, economic and political life in Jamaica."

I will just say here that he evidently understood the culture very well.

Pre-teen Recollections

I knew very little of my ancestry as neither of my parents spoke to me about their parents and grandparents. Knowledge of my father's family was restricted to Gangang and the Stewart family. My godmother Flora's family, who lived nearby, may have been relatives of my grandmother. My mother's birth certificate informs that she was born on August 28, 1905 at Rousseau Road, St. Andrew, to Everard Charles Aaron a reporter, and Leanora Rebecca Aaron nee Hart. Mama occasionally traveled to nearby Spanish Town, the original capital of Jamaica, to visit the Forrester and

Browne families of her two married sisters. I cannot recall their returning a visit to our home. I accompanied her whenever possible for the excitement of the train ride and for the refreshments I anticipated receiving from my aunts. My uncle, Mr. Browne owned a small farm and my mother would bring home a supply of produce from the farm. On one of our visits, after I had gone to the farm a few times, I noticed that my mother did not go up to the main house as usual, but stopped at a small one bedroom house nearer the gate. That was where my aunt was now living. I later heard the rumor that my uncle was living in the main house with his former maid, who was much younger than my aunt. I felt sorry for my aunt and disappointed that I didn't always get to meet my cousins, *Barry** and *Caulder**, who were still living in the main house.

My other aunt, Mrs. Forrester, lived a short distance up the Sligoville road from the highway, before you cross the bridge to enter Spanish Town. I also vaguely recall accompanying my mother to visit a woman whose home was located near Half Way Tree in Kingston. My sister Fay contributes that she was "Mama's relative who gave us tea and cookies. She had mango trees and other fruit growing in her yard and we partook freely. She had two daughters; one was kind and the other beastly to her 'poor' relations"

My family life in the formative years was fraught with prejudice, sadness, favoritism and despair. There were good, joyous, victorious moments too, but those were few. Some of the stories I do not recall personally, but accounts of some of the episodes shared with me by my siblings leave me with feelings that are less than joyous. I do not necessarily doubt the veracity of their recollections, but I must confess that I was somewhat oblivious to much of it and perhaps even blind-sighted by the love I held so dearly for my mother. I have one brother and six sisters. In chronological order, there came Norma, Robert, June, Marjorie, me, Laura, Sheila and Fay.

Very highly influential in our growing up years was my grandmother Gangang. My memory of Gangang elicits a short, slender, old woman of light-brown complexion and stern looking face with a deeply lined forehead. I thought of her as a wicked witch whose main endeavor was to cast evil spells on my mother. My resentment of her unfair treatment to her own grandchildren and her unrelenting disrespect of my mother grew into a fierce hatred of her. My sister June was Gangang's favorite for many years, probably because she had the lightest complexion of all her grandchildren. June is the only one of the eight children who has fond memories of her childhood since she received special and exclusive treatment from Gangang. She recalls that she spent a lot of time at home with Gangang in her relatively spacious, comfortable premises, and often partook of the adequate evening meals Gangang prepared for Papa and herself. Coming home from school, she would often go directly into Gangang's domain for more affection and comfort than she could expect from her mother and siblings. She recalls that Gangang pampered her and taught her to make patchwork sheets from pieces of cloth. At night, she often slept in Gangang's bed. Consequently, she never developed a close relationship with any of her sisters or brothers.

Marjorie was the darkest of the eight siblings and I suspect that my grandmother was responsible for her being sent away from infancy to live with Baba, whom I assumed was a family member. She returned home when she was about seven years old. I do not recall that my youngest sister Fay also lived away from the family during early childhood; however, Fay spoke of this during my visit to New York in July 2009. She told me that she has no memory of her early life before she returned to live with us at age four. Fay also expressed a favorable view of Gangang. She wrote these brief impressions of her. "She was old and infirm when I knew her, but I admired how she kept house. She was kind to me. She allowed me to play with her china miniatures because I was always staring at them. I was fascinated by their intricacy and beauty. I think she managed her household well and took care of the duty of caring for her son until she passed on." In stark contrast, was her impression of Papa as "Terrible; he was sort of a shadow, only emerging when Sheila complained about me, and punishing me because of her complaints without finding out if they were justified. At puberty I started to defend myself against Sheila and unforgettable for me, was when I got really angry and threw a chair at Papa. As an adult, I thought it prudent to acknowledge that he was my father and I should let go of that anger, so I started sending him gifts and money".

I was deeply saddened by Fay's unfortunate impressions of Mama. She stated, "I have two vivid memories. The first was probably when I came back from whatever relations I was staying with from birth. I kept following her around crying while she kept pushing me away. The other happened when I was perhaps 4 old. I went to the outhouse bathroom early in the morning when it was still dark. I thought I saw a male and the presence made me feel safe, secure and at peace. So I told her about it, thinking wonderful thoughts. However, she cautioned me not to trust strangers and reported the incident to the police. Generally, she stayed as far away from me as she could, only emerging to walk behind me to make sure I was in school. Perhaps that is too harsh because she did get me transferred to St. Josephs Girls School when I expressed interest. She was also instrumental in getting me into Alpha Academy even though they rejected me at first. One other memory that stands out is taking a walk with her on the seashore at an early hour. Unforgettable was the beauty of the sands, the waves and the rising sun.

As an adult her relationship with me did not change but I remember one thing she said when I had sent her some gifts that Sheila delivered without telling her it was from me – I asked if the clothing fit and if she liked them. She replied, "It is the ones you do not like that help you." To my mind, the comment seemed to imply the very opposite of what Fay evidently believed; but she was fixed in her view, so I left it alone.

If only in her mind and through her actions, Gangang established a three-tiered social stratum within the home itself. She and her son became the aristocracy. Her fair-skinned grandchildren and Stewart family members were middle class, and my mother low class. There were three separate households living at 11 Highholborn Street as according to the Jamaican census; note that a household is one in which meals are prepared for the members living in that arrangement (Statin). The Stewart family had a large zinc-covered shed in the backyard where they prepared meals. Mama prepared meals for herself and her children on a brick shelf in the yard. Gangang cooked exclusively for herself and Papa in her kitchen. They ate alone in her dining room on copious amounts of good food with meat and vegetables. Gangang would offer any leftovers to her current favorite grandchild. The original choice was Norma, the eldest, followed by the second girl June, and finally Sheila, all of whom were very fair.

During the 1940s my family became extremely poor and very isolated. The salary my father earned as a typesetter at the Gleaner Company, publishers of Jamaica's daily newspaper, was totally inadequate to take care of his mother, his wife and eight children. Yet, he never seemed to have a care in the world. Mama's early education had been sporadic as she was kept home from school on many occasions due to financial constraints. Despite these setbacks, she did well at elementary school and went on to study at a commercial school. Still, her financial contribution from part-time jobs was not significant enough to enable the upward mobility of the family. She stayed home most of the time to take care of her children and with eight of us, she was pregnant or nursing a child much of the time.

She cooked for herself and her eight children in a small open space in the yard between Gangang's kitchen and the zinc-enclosed shower. The only facility it provided was a small brick shelf that could barely hold a coal stove and a few pots. There was hardly ever enough food to satisfy our hunger. We usually ate the same type of meal without any meat for most of the week. Since the weekly house money she received from Papa's salary was woefully inadequate, Mama would go to the Coronation market each weekend. She would buy as much as she could afford of whatever was in excess supply and therefore very cheap. If there was a glut of yam and cabbage in the market we were served these two items exclusively for dinner over many days. As much as she tried to make the food last until the next allowance, however, there were days when there was no money and no food left. Then she would credit white rice, counter flour and sugar from the Chinese shop on the corner. The flour was used to make boiled or fried dumplings, the sugar for sweetening mint tea, sugar-water and limeade. Customers' accounts were recorded in an exercise book and the 'chinie-man' was willing to wait a few weeks until you could pay.

I remember a period when Mama reared chickens from which we obtained eggs for our breakfast. Occasionally, one would end up in our plates for Sunday dinner. The preparation exercise was a gruesome, striking one. The body of the chicken was held down under a large pot with the neck and head extending on the outside. The head was chopped off with a single stroke of a sharp machete and the pot removed for onlookers to see the 'death dance,' as the headless body of the chicken fluttered around the yard for about a minute before it became lifeless. I sometimes helped to remove all the feathers prior to seasoning and cooking the chicken, but I cannot recall the details of how this task was accomplished.

Like my father I am also short, slim and fair-skinned but not as handsome or as 'white.' I do not remember much about my early childhood life, probably because it was mostly an unpleasant experience for me. I had a miserable childhood; lacking in care and affection, with inadequate food to eat and few new clothes to wear. Much of our clothes were hand-me-downs or used clothes obtained from the Salvation Army. Significantly, I cannot recall ever being hugged or kissed by anyone in my immediate family. Nor do I remember any displays of affection between my mother and father.

In fact, there was very little love or affection in my family, which had a rigid hierarchical structure. My grandmother was the czar of the home, my father the prince who followed her edicts, and was never allowed to forget his cardinal sin of marrying the 'no-good black girl.' My grandmother thought herself of superior social standing to all her neighbors, who were black and poor, did not associate with any of them and commanded us not to have anything to do with them. She, and my father to a lesser extent, did not even have a nodding acquaintance with the majority of residents on the street. Our family spoke the "Queens English" and the children were forbidden to speak "Jamaican Patois" in the home. Most of our neighbors spoke only patois and we conversed with them in patois on the street and in school. We were always conscious that we were citizens of "Jamaica up," exiled in a foreign country, "Jamaica down."

My attendance at Miss Knibb's 'infant school' nearby on Tower Street is my earliest recollection of my childhood. The school consisted of a few wooden benches under a zinc-covered shed in the front yard. All the pupils sat together on different benches according to age and knowledge. Beginners were taught the alphabet and numbers. Advanced students were eventually introduced to reading, multiplication and division. Mrs. Valerie Bolt, who recognized me in July 2009 at a dinner and dance cruise at New York Harbor to raise funds for Immaculate High School in Kingston, told me that she graduated from Alpha Academy High School in the same class as my sister June. Her family lived on Water Lane about forty yards south of our home. She advised me that we both attended Miss Nicholas' infant school at Ladd Lane, one block east of Highholborn Street. However, I believe she may have mistaken me for my brother Robert who I reckoned was of similar age to her. Valerie related that her father, who migrated from Cuba to Jamaica, made homemade ice cream for a living. He stored the ice cream in large metal canisters, placed them on ice in his multicolored wooden cart on wheels, and pushed the cart to the downtown commercial area, selling the ice cream along the way. He parked the cart at a busy intersection until all the ice cream was sold. He then returned home to make more ice cream, which he sold outside his gate. In addition to residents in the neighborhood, well-to-do customers patronized him while driving home from their workplaces. I had a realization that I would not have known the ice-cream man, though he lived so near, because ice-cream was a luxury that my family could not afford.

At seven years old, I started attending the Holy Family Elementary School, also called East Branch, operated by the Sisters of Mercy Catholic nuns. I can vividly recall the quarrel about my going to school barefooted that my parents had beside the cistern in the front yard. I was about eight years old by then and my mother had sent me to school without shoes for several days since the hand-me-down canvas shoes I had been wearing had fallen apart. As soon as she realized this was happening, my grandmother informed my father when he came home from work. Papa accosted Mama by the water pipe where she was washing dirty dishes and pots.

"Have you been sending Peter to school barefoot?" he asked. "Yes" she answered.

"I will not have my son going to school barefoot. Don't let it happen again," he shouted at her angrily. I was leaving the toilet to go upstairs but strong feelings of alarm and concern for my mother suddenly overwhelmed me. My heart was beating fast and my feet were transfixed to the ground. Mama slowly wiped her hands, stood erect, turned around and stepped forward to face him. "He has to go to school" she replied firmly,

"And I will continue to send him to school barefoot until you buy shoes for him."

My heart beat faster from a sense of doom that some harm was about to happen to Mama. Papa's body stiffened, his lips tightened and his hands turned into fists. Defiantly, Mama held her ground looking straight into his eyes. I held my breath for what seemed like minutes until his fingers re-opened and his body relaxed.

"I will see what I can do to buy his shoes at the end of the month" he said slowly and softly. Then he turned away and went through Gangang's front door. A sense of relief flooded through me as I ran to hug Mama tightly around her legs.

A few weeks later I received a new pair of Jamaica manufactured Bata canvas shoes. I was grateful for the shoes, as the hot pavement used to burn the soles of my feet on my way home from school in the early afternoon.

I was totally amazed that my meek, downtrodden, abused mother, who had never complained of the daily ill-treatment, disrespect and neglect she suffered from her husband and his mother, had vehemently defied their dictates in order to keep me going to school. Although I did not, at that time, realize the significance of this incident on my life, it was probably a critical, transformational experience that implanted deep into my psyche, a passion for learning and the conviction that education was the vehicle which I could use to take me on a journey from the ghetto, poverty and misery into a place of comfort, abundance and happiness. From this early age I felt challenged and committed to achieve a good education.

This incident no doubt, also contributed to the passion I have always felt for women's rights and the need I have to help women in distress, particularly those who have been taken advantage of by family members. It is no coincidence that my two long-term romantic relationships are with women who had strong, neurotic feelings of resentment against male family members who they perceived took unfair advantage of them. I felt instant chemistry at first sight for, and quickly fell in love with both of them on learning their distress stories. Then I dedicated my life to helping them to be the best and happiest that they could be. I now realize that the helplessness and frustration I felt by my inability to help my mistreated mother was perhaps the main reason for my childhood sadness. This has embedded deep within me, a subconscious, innate need to assist and care for women in distressed circumstances to make up for my failure to help my mother.

I attended Holy Family Elementary School from the mid-1940s to early-50s. In July 2012, Rupert Johnson wrote a letter to the Daily Gleaner newspaper describing 'what transpired in the field of elementary education during the 1940s and 50s.'

He noted that elementary schools were divided into three divisions:

"The Lower Division was subdivided into three classes, Junior A, Junior B and First Class; the Middle Division two classes, Second and Third Standards, and the Upper Division Fourth, Fifth and Sixth Standards ...

According to my recollection, both teachers and pupils in small elementary schools, with a population 200 or fewer, suffered immeasurably.

In the Lower Division, all three classes were generally taught by one fully trained or partially trained teacher. She was sometimes assisted by an untrained teacher, usually a pupil teacher or a probationer. The probationer was one who held the Third Year Jamaica Local Exam certificate and was put on probation for a six-year period.

The pupil teacher was below the rank of the probationer. This was a trainee who had passed the Second-Year Jamaica Local Exam and was preparing to take the Third-Year Exam.

In many instances, the entire Middle Division was taught by a probationer, The Upper Division was invariably taught by the head teacher.

Each teacher had to teach all subjects, namely: reading, written English, arithmetic, scripture, geography/history, science, physical education, music and handwork.'

Note: The Jamaica Local Exams were taken by the brightest elementary school students who were denied the opportunity to attend private high school.

The first government-built secondary schools in Jamaica would come only in 1961 (Morant Bay High and St Mary High) - the year before political independence. Despite her extremely adverse circumstances, my mother was determined that her children should receive a good education. To this end, she displayed exceptional drive, ingenuity, fortitude and self-sacrifice.To send her children to school she did a variety of part-time jobs both inside and outside the home. I don't remember Mama speaking very much to me. I suppose that she was much too busy trying to keep her numerous children clothed, fed and in school. Her few words were usually about what was happening that day and how I was doing in school. She constantly urged us to pay attention at school, do our homework, study and read books. By following her advice, I came first in A, B, and C Classes at the Catholic Holy Family Elementary School. However, I could not be promoted from C class because of a Ministry of Education rule stating that to be promoted from C Class, you had to be of a certain age, which I had not yet attained. The better students from C Class did not go into First Class since that was reserved for C Class students who had not done well and for new entrants close in age to the Second Class age threshold. I was very disappointed to hear that I would have to repeat C Class while my classmates went on to Second Class. My eldest sister, Norma, accompanied me to the headmistress to object to my being kept back. She enquired if the rule prevented my skipping from C Class to Third Class the following year to rejoin my former classmates. She was told that, although it was permitted by the rule, I would not be able to manage Third Class work without Second Class preparation.

The following year I was placed in Second Class. My sister Norma returned to Sister Philomena to request that I be put into Third Class to rejoin my original classmates. I was very impressed with Norma's boldness and particularly pleased that she would take this action for my benefit. I thought that she was demonstrating that she loved and cared for me. I treasured that moment from then until now, and will always be grateful to my eldest sister for her actions, which meant so much to me at that time. At Norma's dogged insistence the headmistress agreed to try me in Third Class, although she doubted that I could manage. I wondered if I would be able to cope in Third Class. I silently vowed that I would try to justify my sister's faith in me and do the best I could possibly do. With a great deal of effort, I not only coped from the start, but also came first in the Third Class final examinations and first in every other class thereafter.

In the 1950s, there were very few high and secondary schools in Jamaica, with spaces for less than 10% of the total children of secondary school age. Most were private, church affiliated schools whose fees only affluent families could afford. There were two government technical secondary schools. Kingston Technical School had its beginning in 1896 as a model school to offer "Advanced Manual Training", in the hope that it would develop into "a centre of good General and Technical Education".

In 1912, advanced instruction in Woodwork, Metalwork and Home Economics was being given to teachers who were expected to pass on the skills in the communities where they worked.

In the 1920s tailoring, shoe-making, carpentry and metalwork were added in special classes. During the 1950s and 1960s, the school provided upgrading courses for Shorthand Typists in the Civil Service. My eldest sister, Norma, attended Kingston Technical School for the Shorthand and Typist training. My brother Robert was enrolled by Mama into an inexpensive, unregistered secondary school and used most of the little spare time she could find to supervise his school work. I was jealous of my brother receiving most of my mother's care and attention especially since he was performing poorly while I excelled in my schoolwork. In his final year she paid the registration fees for the British overseas exams and accompanied Robert to the examination center every day. After the results of the exams were available Mama visited the school and was heartbroken to learn that he had not passed a single subject. He probably had left the exam room sometimes soon after she did, because he had not submitted any answers for some subjects.

When I was 12 years old, the age for entering Jamaican high schools, my family had no funds to send me to one of the more affordable, unregistered secondary schools used by ambitious families with limited funds. I was not aware of any scholarship opportunities and never thought that there was any possibility of my attending a high school. However, Sister Philomena, the headmistress of my school, thought that I was too intelligent to be denied a high school education. She proposed that I should teach arithmetic to younger students in 'extra classes' after regular school hours for one shilling per week per student. She would keep all the fees until there were enough funds to pay for a year's tuition in high school.

During elementary school, I had a special relationship with two girls. I was distracted from my studies by my younger sister, Laura, and attracted to the other, an elementary schoolmate, Marie Wiles*. Laura is only one year and five months younger than me, and was a willful, mischievous child. She selected me to be her companion in some of her truant escapades. She occasionally persuaded me, after we left home for school, to explore instead, various parts of Kingston. Our favorite locations were the seashore at Breezy Castle nearby and Hope Botanical Gardens, which was once a sugar plantation. The Hope Gardens was certainly my favorite spot in Kingston during my childhood and I made many enjoyable visits there.

Lady Nugent's description of Hope Garden appears in the book, 'Jamaica':

> "Conversion into the most beautiful botanical garden in the West Indies began around the middle of the nineteenth century. Two hundred acres are under cultivation. The central section is laid out for decorative effect, amply achieved by means of exotic plants of every description. The display of orchids is notably rich, and so are the collection of palms and cacti. The outskirts are occupied by a chain of experimental stations, where fruit and other economic trees, timber, and ornamental shrubs are grown. Seedlings in pots made out of bamboo joints are sold to the public at very low prices. No outdoor resort is more popular with residents. Nearly all tourists are taken there."

Marie Wiles* sat behind me in my second year of C class and noticed that I was very quiet, and in particular didn't speak to any of the girls at school. Liking the company of boys and being mischievous, she apparently decided that she would make me speak to her and become her friend. She first tried speaking to me. When I did not respond, she tried other means of gaining my attention, including pricking my arm with a pin, hitting me lightly with her ruler and pulling my hair, all the while with a smile. That certainly got my attention. I must have realized that she wanted us to be friends and I began to converse with her at school.

Nevertheless, I didn't visit her home, which was only a few blocks from my home, nor did I ever invite her to visit mine. However, when her family moved about a mile away to Jones Town, she invited me to visit her new home. I received a warm welcome, was served refreshments by her mother and was very happy that I went. I looked forward to visiting again, always enjoyed the times I spent there, and felt more comfortable than in my family's home.

On one of our escapades, Laura and I left home for school but diverted to a popular section of the Rae Town seashore called Breezy Castle. We stripped to our underwear and went into the sea to bathe. I wandered too far offshore, stepped over an underwater shelf and found myself suddenly standing in deeper water, higher than my head. I thrashed about frantically. Luckily, I soon found higher ground and was able to breathe again. I ran home wet and we got a rare beating from Papa that evening for our truancy. I am still a little fearful of swimming in the sea even though I subsequently learned how to swim.

I do not recall much of my pre-teen childhood life at home, perhaps because it contained too many unpleasant experiences and heartaches. I do remember being so unhappy that I often sat alone at the bottom of the staircase in the night, crying silently for no particular reason but for my strong feelings against the poverty, discrimination and injustice in my home and my community. Particularly upsetting was the constant disrespect and verbal abuse showered on Mama by Gangang. I hated Gangang with a raging passion. I was furious with Papa for not supporting Mama. I lost respect, but could not feel hate for him. I felt helpless and frustrated that I could not defend my mother. My anger grew until I felt that my heart could burst under its pressure. One night, sitting at the bottom of the stairs alone in the darkness, I was so overcome with sadness that I cried and cried for what seemed like hours. I sobbed until I ran out of tears, or so it seemed to me. This time, however, my mind cleared of hopelessness and became filled with the resolve to help my mother somehow, sometime. I vowed to find a way to help Mama and to take her away from Papa and Gangang as soon as I possibly could.

Mama must also have been trying to find her own way out of the darkness also, as I have vague memories of her being involved in the political activities taking place in the forties and fifties. Alexander Bustamante, founder and president of the Bustamante Industrial Trade Union (B.I.T.U.) often held his trade union meetings with the dockworkers nearby our home. On several occasions I witnessed his tall, striking, commanding figure striding up Highholborn Street past our home ahead of a noisy crowd of B.I.T.U. members on their way to the meetings. My mother was at one time a member of the local political group supporting the People's National Party (PNP). I would sometimes follow her to PNP political meetings, attended by large numbers of people, held on the streets of our neighborhood. I do not think anything came of those meetings where mama's upward mobility was concerned and she may have given it up.

The southwest street corner, north of our home also served as the meeting place of several different denominations for their religious services. There was a large area of sidewalk in front of the grocery shop, which was closed on Sundays. Maybe due to its philanthropic nature, the Salvation Army services were always well attended and usually took the form of prayers, a sermon and the singing of hymns, followed by a collection.

But the highlight of my formative years is centered on that very short period in December, known as the 'Christmas holiday. I can vividly remember Christmas as a time of excitement and wonder. Most large businesses and wealthy employers gave Christmas bonuses ranging from one week to one month's additional pay to their employees. (Of course, I did not know that at the time.) Consequently, the employees had extra money to spend on their families during the Christmas and New Year holiday periods. On Christmas Eve, we would go to bed excited with the anticipation of waking early on Christmas morning to see if Santa Claus had brought us a present, provided that we had behaved ourselves throughout the year. Financed by my father's bonus payment, we would awake on Christmas morning to find what Santa Claus had brought us during the night. It was usually an item of clothing. On Christmas Day, dressed in our new clothes and perhaps, with a few pennies in our pockets, we would walk to the downtown-shopping district between Church Street and Orange Street. King Street was aptly named, since it reigned as the premier shopping center of Kingston.

It presented a spectacular sight at Christmas time. All its shops were lit up and decorated in a kaleidoscope of colors. Numerous street venders offered clothes, food, toys, trinkets, balloons, firecrackers and thunderbolts, among other items. The streets and nearby Victoria Park were crowded with adults shopping and their children clutching balloons and toys. The entire downtown area reverberated with cries of merriment by children, venders hawking their wares, the rat-a-tat of firecrackers and the boom of the occasional thunderbolt.

The *Jonkunnu* parades during the Christmas holiday season created much excitement for the young children. Jonkunnu was a traditional dance form of African descent that linked music, dance, symbols and mime. The dancers wore costumes depicting characters; among the principal of which were the Devil, the Horse Head, Pitchy Patchy, the King, the Queen, the Policeman, and Big Belly Woman. They were attired in elaborate costumes with headdresses, masks, pitchforks, batons, and other paraphernalia associated with their characters. They were accompanied by drummers and danced through the streets in time with the beat of the drums. They occasionally made threatening moves towards the onlookers, which precipitated screams from the children. The more timid ran and hid behind the adults, emerging again only after the parade had passed. However, by the beginning of the twenty first century the Jonkunnu dancers were rarely seen in the capital city of Kingston and today are usually only seen in cultural fairs and rural parts of the island.

Beside this one great annual event, there were few recreational opportunities for the rest of the year and especially at home. But as children will always be, especially poor ones in an environment devoid of technology from the most commonplace item such as a television to the more exotic such as ipads and cell phones, which were unheard of at the time, we devised our own forms of entertainment. We spun gigs, played hopscotch and games of marbles outside our gate. Inside, we played tic-tac-toe and card games, of which I remember donkey, coon can and strip-me-naked. Skipping was the most popular pastime activity since it required minimal, inexpensive equipment and could be played by a single individual or a group. Group skipping was often accompanied by chanting ditties. Examples are: 'Mosquito 1, mosquito 2, mosquito jump into hot callaloo' and 'room for rent apply within, when one moves out, one moves in.'

We climbed trees to the roof of the furniture-making shop next door, flew homemade kites, rode the tram car that passed by our home and occasionally visited the nearby Breezy Castle beach on Sundays. The hand-cranked Victrola Gramophone provided music until it stopped working. For a short period we were able to afford Rediffusion; the speaker box for which you paid a small monthly rental, which was an economical way of listening to the Radio Jamaica and Rediffusion (RJR) radio-broadcasts.

The tramcar was a public transportation open-sided vehicle that ran on rails and was powered by overhead electric lines. The tramway service served the residential areas of the Kingston corporate area and formed a link with the railway service to Montego Bay and Port Antonio. Kingston's first electric line was incorporated on 31 March 1899, and the entire system was closed on May 10, 1948. The Jamaica Public Service Company claimed that it could not afford to maintain the right-of-way or conduct needed extensions. There were several routes, one of which, the Rockfort Gardens line, passed by our home on Highholborn Street making a loud, rattling noise that could be heard from far away. This was the most exciting daily event in our lives and I usually ran outside to watch it pass by.

One day, while racing over the uneven yard stones to catch sight of the tramcar before it passed, I tripped, fell headlong and suffered a long gash under my chin that bled profusely. I was rushed to the hospital. The cut required many stitches and I retained a prominent scar under my chin for many years into adulthood. On Sundays when the tram was crowded, we occasionally hopped onto the moving car. We rode it around to Fleet Street two blocks from home and sometimes longer without paying the fare. If the conductor asked us to show our tickets, we quickly jumped off the tram and walked back home.

As the stories show, ingenuity was a way of life for us, even at that tender age. Another ingenious way of expanding our entertainment options was our occasional visits to the cinema. The Gaiety and Palace cinemas on East Queen Street were only a short walking distance away from home; however, we rarely saw a movie since we could not afford the entrance fee. My cousin Jackie reminded me that we sometimes gained entrance to the Palace Theatre between the first and second shows by walking backwards into the theater through the wide exit gate while the first show patrons were leaving.

But of all the forms of entertainment or indulgences, my favorite was my visits to the Institute of Jamaica. We regularly visited this cultural center comprising a branch of the national library, an art collection, a science museum, a history gallery and a small zoo; situated only a few blocks away at the corners of East and Tower Streets. I read voraciously at the Junior Library, sometimes finishing two or three novels in a single day.

And so, the foregoing encapsulates my recollection of my pre-teen years. Generally speaking, I was underfed, unhappy, confused, bright and creative, but rebellious. Something that was of great importance to me was to do well at school. In an attempt to escape from the harsh realities of life, I spent a large portion of my free time reading books at the Junior Library of the Institute of Jamaica. At home and in my community I was confronted with poverty, discrimination, prejudice and injustice as a way of life. I was keenly watching the behavior of my parents, siblings, neighbors, teachers and priests, who were interacting with each other in various and contrasting ways. I noticed the great disparities in housing, facilities, food, clothing, education, recreation, personal respect and disrespect in every sphere of life, and wondered why there was such a great divide. A simple personal example to contemplate is that the children would be hungry while our grandmother and father were feasting on adequate, kitchen cooked, hot meals in the comfort of her dining room.

What I was taught in Sunday school about the life and teaching of Jesus made me begin to wonder if the discriminatory practices at home, in my community and throughout Jamaica were the right and proper things to do. It was difficult for me as a child to resolve these conflicting messages and experiences, and it made me temperamental and unhappy. I was probably most influenced to reject a path of discrimination and injustice for my life by the outrage I felt in seeing the extreme disrespect, disadvantages and injustices inflicted on my mother. I must have begun to realize that certain accepted practices in my family, community and country were not in keeping with the commandments of God and the ministry of Jesus Christ. I felt instinctively that they were wrong and were to be rejected.

From these early years, I felt that I could not trust that what people thought, said, and acted, were automatically right. Surely, my grandmother's discriminatory treatment of my mother was not in keeping with my religious teaching in Sunday school. Jesus Christ said, "Love thy neighbor as thyself. Do good to those who hate you." My grandmother represented the chief authority in my life. I felt very strongly that some of her beliefs, instructions and actions were at best misguided and at worst evil. Therefore, I began to distrust authority and to develop resistance to whomever in authority advocated behavior that was discriminatory and contrary to the teachings of

Christ. Later on in my teenage and early years of adulthood, I learned that certain accepted beliefs and practices of the Jamaican society, and some of Jamaica's laws, were also discriminatory and contrary to the teachings of Christ, and therefore ought to be resisted. I was challenged to understand why there was so much abuse and injustice in the world.

In Jamaica, if you were black and poor, you were powerless and usually lacking any opportunity to achieve a better life for yourself and your family. Even the few prosperous black families felt they were superior to the poor black majority and mimicked the colonial value system.

In the *Sunday Gleaner* of February 16, 2014, Dr. Carolyn Cooper relates why the Jamaican Rhodes Scholar, Stuart Hall, who left in 1951 to go to Oxford University, never returned to Jamaica. At an interview in 1997, Caryl Philips, another Oxford man, asked Hall, "Why did you choose not to go back?" He gave two answers. "There was no need to hurry back …… But there's a second which is more personal. You see, I came from this peculiar colored middle class …. I didn't want to go back to that. I couldn't bear it. I'd always meant to go home, but I'd always had reservations about becoming a member of that class." Hall did another interview in 2007 with journalist Tim Adams, during which he explained why he chose not to return. "I was always the blackest member of my family and I knew it from the moment my sister said: 'Where did you get this coolie baby from?' Cultural studies were born for me when I was told I could not bring black school friends home, even though, to white eyes, I was black myself."

Tragically, many of the poor, black majority also believed that they were inferior to both the whites and the fair-skinned mulattoes. The advantages of a lighter skin were evident, particularly in achieving higher social status and superior job opportunities. Consequently, many Jamaicans sought to lighten their skin color by various methods, the chief of which is the use of bleaching creams on their skin. Dr. Persadsingh, who has written extensively against the practice, reported in the *Gleaner,* a Jamaican newspaper, in an article which appeared November 15, 2009, that "Skin bleaching has become socially accepted and the practice is connected to deep-rooted issues of identity and self-image with which many Jamaicans continue to wrestle." He says, "Even in today's society, many Jamaicans equate being white, brown or fair with success and beauty. Next to skin color, hair was the determining feature of your status, especially for females. Long, straight "good" hair indicated beauty and upper class. Short, kinky "bad" hair condemned her as ugly and lower class."

In her autobiography, *Growing Out*, Barbara Blake Hannah writes, "Hair was so very important as I grew up. Hair was the dividing line between white and black, between pretty and ugly, between upper and lower class.

How I wished for a trace of straight in my natty profusion. At boarding school my sister and I would be excused from lunch...to wash and comb our hair. The pain of comb-out was awful, the humiliation worse. Ninety percent of the girls at my very top-drawer boarding school were white... and from rich families, all a constant parade of envy-making hair beauty. I knew I could never have such hair and bore the mark of my inferiority with resignation."

Sadly many Jamaicans of both sexes continue to believe that if they have fairer skin and straighter hair, it will be easier for them to get a job, get married and live a happy life." Unfortunately, there is daily evidence that their belief is true to this day.

CHAPTER TWO

Teenage Recollections and Reflections

My teenage memories are dominated by the sexual urges I felt and repressed because of my belief in the Catholic Church's doctrine that sex before marriage was a mortal sin. I was increasingly attracted to girls, but was always afraid to approach them or to take any action to indicate that I liked them. Besides, I was concentrating on my schoolwork and after-school teaching job from which I never received any money to spend. I was conscious of and perhaps ashamed of wearing used clothes from the Salvation Army. I probably thought that I was unattractive to girls and had no means of entertaining them. However, at home I found a way to relieve the peaks of sexual urges I often felt. The bathroom consisted of a shower head for cold water near the recessed end of the house wall. It was enclosed on top and the other three sides entirely by zinc sheets on a wooden frame with a door facing the walkway. The small space between the recessed wall and the shower was used by my mother to cook our meals. No one could see inside this makeshift 'kitchenette' unless they stood directly in front of the open space between the wall and the shower.

Whenever I was feeling a sexual urge, I would watch for one of the girls going to take a shower. Then I would slip undetected into the 'kitchenette' to look through one of the larger peepholes in the zinc to watch the show. Unwittingly, they would provide me with a great strip tease which I enjoyed; starting from the taking off the dress over their head to the stepping out of their panties. In deep anticipation, I unzipped my pants and held my penis in my hands, caressing it gently. It brought exquisite pleasure to view them soaping their body especially the bottom, the breasts and the vagina. By this time my penis was very stiff and throbbing. By squeezing my penis a few times I would induce ejaculation and welcome relief. Luckily, I was never caught as I was very cautious and even when aroused, paid keen attention to listen. Whenever I heard someone approaching, I would quickly zip up my pants and step outside. If any of the girls knew I was watching them they never mentioned it to me.

I remember once that I moved when watching one of my cousins. My foot touched the zinc and made a sound. Turning off the shower, she spun around to look intently towards me. I stepped back and held my breath; fearful I had been discovered. However, she soon continued her shower. A happy sense of relief washed over me as I started breathing again. When I resumed watching she started humming a tune as if nothing had happened. Perhaps she suspected that someone was watching but decided that she didn't mind being watched after all.

Beside my sexual escapades, the other thoughts dominating my recollection again relates to social interactions, injustices and prejudices, both at home and societal. Although my family was fair-skinned, we were too poor to be welcomed into the prosperous fair-skinned or even the black middle classes. Therefore, since my family remained aloof from the poor black people in our community, they were excluded from every social structure. I can't recall my father having any friends, nor was I aware that he had any girlfriends outside his marriage. He went to work during weekdays and came home to read his Gleaner newspaper, smoke his pipe and listen to the radio broadcast. On Saturdays, he sometimes went alone to horseracing at Race Course in central Kingston. On Sundays, the family walked to Catholic morning service at the Holy Trinity Cathedral on North Street about a quarter-mile from home.

My mother never complained about the unfair and demeaning treatment she received from her mother-in-law and, to a lesser extent, from her husband. She appeared to accept her life as it was. She knew the kind of persons my grandmother and father were, knew that they were not going to change and resigned herself to accept the situation for the sake of her children. She treated them with respect and selflessly did the work of fulfilling the needs of her children as best she could. She usually accepted their dictates unless she perceived that it would be detrimental to her children's education, then the claws came out and she stood her ground defiantly.

She was determined to provide the best care for her children that she could manage with very inadequate resources and also to give them the best education that she could afford. To this end, she tried to supplement the meager weekly allowance my father gave her with part-time employment of various kinds. I remember her working part-time as an office maid and operating a home school in the yard for children in the neighborhood. I felt strongly that my mother was being mistreated and taken advantage of. I felt rebellious and unhappy about the situation, and frustrated that I could do nothing to help her.

My mother's interest in others was not confined to her own children. She had a kind word and a helping hand for everyone in need. She saw only the good in people and encouraged them to improve themselves. She maintained that all work had dignity and should be done to the best of one's ability. She especially displayed consideration for the poor neighborhood children. She taught shorthand and typing skills to many teenage girls for a small fee or no fee if they could no longer pay. I have the highest regard for my mother, whom I consider kind, compassionate, and dedicated to her children's welfare, particularly their education. My sister Sheila shares my opinion to the extent that she proposed in 2006, that our family fund a scholarship program in my mother's honor to assist needy Jamaican students. The idea came to her when a woman approached her in New York City and asked her if she was related to Mrs. Muir who lived on Highholborn Street in Jamaica. On hearing that Sheila was her daughter the woman stated that our mother had taught her secretarial skills. She attributed her success to our mother's teaching, advice and encouragement.

Laura, however, does not share our high regard for our mother. She strongly believes that Mama is totally undeserving of any honor, and refused to contribute to the scholarship fund. She says that her most vivid recollection of Mama is returning home with her after purchasing groceries from the nearby 'chinie-man' shop. Mama saw a handkerchief floating in dirty water from recent rain in the gutter of Highholborn Street. She picked it up in full view of neighbors and pedestrians walking by. Laura was embarrassed and mortified and apparently lost whatever respect she had for Mama from then until this day. She was also distressed that Mama made her wear used clothes from the Salvation Army. Mama died of a heart attack on September 6, 1984. More details about her final years will be provided in the sequel *"Lifelong Learning: Your Sure Path to Good Health and Financial Success"*. To a materialistic world, she was just a poor, simple, black woman of little or no consequence. However, to me, her strong faith in God, her thirst for knowledge, her positive attitude to work, her compassion for her neighbors and her dedication to her children made her a truly outstanding person and a wonderful role model.

My mother's acceptance of the prejudice, discrimination and injustice she suffered was reflected in the hearts and minds of many poor black citizens in my community, in the capital city of Kingston, in the rural areas and the entire island of Jamaica. The majority of poor black people accepted the colonialist philosophy that Caucasian people were superior to Negroes, that they were more intelligent, more civilized, more skilled and better leaders. Therefore, most Jamaicans accepted that white people were born to rule while non-whites were born to serve their colonial masters. Prior to Jamaica attaining partial self-government in 1944, those poor blacks that rejected that they were inferior would soon learn that the best opportunities in education, employment and government were reserved for whites only and a few favored mulattoes. Even after full independence in 1962, some of these attitudes and practices still prevailed and have not been totally eradicated to this day. Poor black people knew that the government, the laws, the economy, the education system and the society were structured for the benefit of the ruling and upper classes, while keeping the disadvantaged poor blacks in their inferior status. They were certainly not happy with the state of affairs, but they also knew that there was very little, if anything, that they could do about it. In the past, the authorities had dealt ruthlessly with all attempts at organized public protests. The police were sent to disperse the crowds and those that resisted were beaten and put in jail.

All these factors led and contributed to my general distrust of authority figures and instilled in me a sense of stubbornness and an intense desire to go against rules and norms even when it would seem to be to my detriment. Defiance had just become a part of my ingrained character. There were many times when this proved to be to my personal detriment and loss; there were others when it proved beneficial.

In 1953, during my first year in high school, I had a serious injury while playing baseball on the school grounds. As I was considered very intelligent by my teachers and peers, I will justify the stupidity of my actions, by saying my intellect had taken a short vacation in my exuberance of playing on a baseball team in a game that I had long wanted to play. So in my excitement, I was standing right behind the batter when a hard incoming ball dislodged the bat from his hand and it connected full blast with my mouth. The unfathomable pain I felt was confirmed by my doctor to be caused by a broken lower jaw bone as well as the dislodging of the two right upper incisor teeth and three lower incisor front teeth. On a subsequent visit he informed me that all five front teeth were dead. I would need to remove them right then, otherwise, they would soon cause pain and damage to my gums as long as they remained as they were. However, I was not feeling any pain from the teeth at that time and decided to disobey his instructions.

Suffice it to say sixty years later, I finally got around to removing them when indeed they proved to be damaging my gums. So I would say there are instances when we must assess a situation and take a decision in our best interest, even if it goes against the opinion or expert advice given.

It should not be hard to imagine what it would have been like as a poor young boy, with no financial capability to replace these missing teeth, to go through life for many years with such a large gaping space at the front of his mouth.

Stormy Weather

"Life's not about waiting for the storm to pass. It's about learning to dance in the rain."
Vivian Greene

On Friday night the 17th of August, 1951, Hurricane Charlie struck Jamaica with all its might – up to 125 miles per hour. Shortly after sunset, the strong winds began and kept us awake in anticipation of the coming storm. Suddenly, in the pitch-blackness of night, the winds increased in speed and ferocity causing the house to creak softly and sway gently. The wind's speed and ferocity seemed to be increasing by the minute and continued for what seemed like hours until the soft creaking became a terrifying shriek and the top of the walls swung to and fro by what seemed more than a yard. From outside we heard eerie tearing, crunching, and loud crashing noises until we became very frightened and feared for our lives. Someone bolted for the door and ran out unto the open verandah. We all dashed outside into the fury of the screaming wind and slashing rain and ran to the staircase, only to find that our large ackee tree had fallen across the stairs blocking our way. Desperate to escape the terror at our backs we unhesitatingly plunged into the tree branches and fought to climb our way down the stairs, ignoring the bumps and scratches we suffered along the way.

As each of us reached the ground, we started banging on the front door downstairs and shouting, "Gangang, open the door, Gangang let us in." We were all finally downstairs banging and shouting for what seemed like an eternity before the door was opened; we all rushed in and the door was closed behind us. Almost immediately afterwards, we heard a gut-wrenching, ear-splitting uproar, which you could imagine would signal the end of the world. However, we were soon to realize that it meant that Charlie had claimed our home as its own. The rain poured through the wooden floor overhead into every room and no one could find even standing room to escape the ever-falling rain. We sought some relief by covering our head and shoulders with a towel and our bodies with sheets. After what seemed like hours, the rain and wind stopped completely. We thought the storm was over and went outside to assess the damage the storm had done to our home and the neighborhood. However, except for standing room outside the front door, the fallen ackee tree completely blocked our way to the yard and the gate. We could only play with its branches until the storm resumed its destructive wrath on Jamaica.

My sister Fay recalls Hurricane Charlie as the most memorable event of her childhood. She wrote to me, "Charlie leveled the second floor. I had a recurrence of whooping cough and water was pouring down through the ceiling. I was covered with something waterproof. Cherry (nickname for Norma) was mostly the one who nursed me. When calm in the middle came, I went outside and climbed in between the branches of the fallen ackee tree and had a great time. When we were evacuated to the shelter, I had an even greater time because other kids were there to play with and I actually ate enough food regularly. I thought corned beef was the greatest".

One can only imagine the misery she experienced during her early childhood, why she can declare that living on a portion of the floor of a temporary storm shelter in a school building, and being fed on government rations, was one of the happiest periods of her entire childhood.

The next morning we wandered outside, tired and bleary-eyed, but thankful that we were still alive. After clearing a path through the ackee tree branches to the gate, we looked up to see the state of our home, but to our disbelief, there was absolutely nothing there. Nothing was left; neither roof, nor wall, nor fixture, nor furniture, nor clothing, nor book, nor food, nothing at all! Yet surprisingly, the Stewarts' adjacent upstairs room was intact, roof and all. We ran out into the street and witnessed a scene of devastation; houses flattened, roofs blown off, trees uprooted, debris everywhere. A lot of people were wandering around looking bewildered. We were to learn that the devastation was spread throughout the length and breadth of Jamaica. Charlie was the most devastating natural disaster to hit Jamaica since the 1907 earthquake, which destroyed Kingston. The island was left reeling with over 150 people dead, 2,000 injured, over 25,000 left homeless and damage estimated at US$60,000,000, with more than 20,000 buildings destroyed, thousands of farms smashed, fishing fleets sunk, drinking water polluted, power lines down and numerous roads blocked.

The homeless were sheltered in the schools and churches still standing, or in shacks built from debris. My family, minus Papa who had moved in with Gangang, was allocated a sheet-sized portion of the floor in the Wesley Elementary School hall on Tower Street, where we lived together with several other homeless families for several months. We received help with food and clothes from relief agencies. The lost rooms at home were not rebuilt; instead a zinc-sheeted roof was built over the exposed downstairs area. The Stewarts eventually moved out and my family moved back home into the two rooms they had vacated; Papa occupied the room upstairs and the rest of us packed into the downstairs room.

My Street Corner Gang

A feature of the poor neighborhoods of Kingston was, and still is, the street corner gangs. In the early 1950s, most of these groups were small, non-violent and crime free; unlike today when the term is synonymous with crime. High school was unavailable and unaffordable; housing sub-standard and crowded, unemployment was rife. As a result, young men were not gainfully engaged in any meaningful way and could always be seen on the streets in large numbers. They spent very little time at home; pausing there only to eat and sleep, but they hardly ever strayed further than a block or two.

Things were no different on my block. Included in this statistical and social grouping, were the males in my family, including me. Here is a dossier of the young men between the ages of fifteen to twenty one living on my street, third block up from the sea, in the1950s. Gene, the eldest, was the only son of devoted parents, the wealthiest family on the block; but he had no ambition and failed to attend high school through the family's lack of interest. Unemployed yet always with money, he had the attention of all the young women in the area.

Opposite Gene's home was ours, with my brother Bobby, my cousin Jackie and me; the youngest. Bobby was a mild-mannered, soft-spoken person who never got into a quarrel or a fight. Snobbery was entirely foreign to his nature; whereas our family prided itself on a social distinction we did not actually possess. My cousin Jackie attended Protestant Wesley Elementary, whereas the other members went to Catholic Holy Family Elementary School. Jackie hardly ever associated with the group, scrupulously avoiding a close relationship with any of the members except Bobby and me. I was several years younger than the others, and only got into the group because I was Bobby's brother.

Below us, Noel lived in one of the many dilapidated and overcrowded tenements in the area. Noel was an only child of unmarried parents who lived together in harmony and faithfulness to each other. They were refined in speech and actions, and presented a striking contrast to the other families, who were constantly quarrelling and fighting amongst themselves and with each other. Noel was handsome and intelligent, but his parents could not afford to send him to high school. Like most of the group members, he had attended Holy Family Elementary where he and Bobby became close friends. It is interesting to note, that because of family pressure on my brother, they would probably not otherwise have become friends, even though they were next-door neighbors.

Brother, the elder son of the Gordon's, was the friendliest person in the group and was liked by everyone despite his attempts at social climbing. He tried to make friends with my older sisters who were considered snobs. Baby was two years younger, but appeared more mature than his brother, nicknamed Brother. He was uncommunicative and reserved, but he impressed girls favorably and had a steady girlfriend to whom he was devoted.

Brammy, whose mother was unmarried and living with a common-law 'husband,' not her son's father, was a conceited young man who liked to think he had a way with girls, and always appeared neatly dressed.

Next door to the tenement yard, Squeaky lived with his older sister and his mother, who seemed too frail to cope with the problems of life. Squeaky was a lot like her, small, thin, and anxious to have someone to lean on.

The group had a fairly stable structure that changed little during my few years of association with it. Actually, the group did not consider itself a street gang, although they congregated daily on the street for many years in spite of stiff opposition to their continued presence. My grandmother dedicated herself to terminating my and Bobby's participation in the group, but she could not shake his friendship with Noel, and I was my brother's disciple. Some of the other gang members' mothers also disapproved of their sons 'living in the street' to no avail. None of the homes, except ours, had any space for the gang to meet. However, Gangang would not permit any of the gang members to enter her home. The group headquarters was situated between my family's home and the "cold supper shop" next door, which the group patronized. From the shop we borrowed four stools and a small table on which to play dominoes, draughts, or card games, or we would just sit and chat. My grandmother would try to disperse us on the pretext of wetting the dust or by complaining of a headache from the noise, so the group was very hostile to her.

The game of dominoes was the chief activity of the group and the most important factor in determining the status of a member in the group. Played between two pairs of partners, it is a game that requires keen concentration and close cooperation with the partner. The rival pairs always played a 'six', that is, a round of games played until a pair of partners won six games, and then the losers would be replaced by another pair, the winning players remaining in the game until they were beaten. Bobby and Noel, the two best players, always played together as partners whenever both were present.

The second most important activity was the game of draughts or Spanish checkers, played by two individuals, one against the other. Both Bobby and Noel were excellent players and were very evenly matched. I was a close rival to the leaders, then came Gene, Brother, Baby, Squeaky, and Brammy, the same positions as for dominoes. Because he lacked the regular practice against better players, I always beat Jackie when we played draughts at home. Even now, when the occasion arises, such as house parties hosted by him, Jackie still relates my prowess in the game of draughts describing in detail how easily I was able to defeat him.

There was very little organization within the structure of the group. Members considered themselves of equal status to each other and would have resisted the attempts of any one member to rule. Out of group interaction, a system of mutual obligations arose which was essential for group cohesion. As the members performed their activities as a unit, numerous occasions arose when they could do favors for one another. A member helped principally in two ways, lending money and treating to a snack at the shop. Noel and Bobby had steady jobs and aided the rest of the group much more than the others could reciprocate, and this helped to strengthen their high status within the group. Although there was no conscious regard to organization, there were nevertheless, distinctions in rank among the group. Noel and Bobby held the top positions, and could be called leaders in a very limited usage of the term. They were older members, and were well known throughout the district for their ability as a team in dominoes and also their skill in draughts. They were also well respected for their intelligence and power of self-expression. Noel was undoubtedly the leading figure of the group. He possessed the greatest degree of proficiency in most of the other varied activities of the group, including cricket, soccer, card games, and dancing skill, and a closer adherence to the norms of the group than Bobby. His family was meek and friendly, whereas Bobby's was hostile and superior.

I must admit to holding an ambivalent attitude toward the group, which I doubt was shared by any other member. Within the group, the members were transformed into my peers and comrades and I was perfectly at ease. But apart from the group, I sometimes felt a sense of superiority toward the group, as well as guilty feelings on account of my membership in the group. No doubt, this was partially due to my family's attitudes and influence. But I was also the only one top of my classes at school and determined to escape from downtown Kingston and poverty. All the other members of the group seemed satisfied with their status in life and their environment. They only required a steady job that could provide the basic necessities of food, clothing and shelter with a little left over for entertaining their male and female friends. I suspect that I wanted more from life than this, although I could not define exactly what that meant. I had a feeling that I did not belong in downtown Kingston and that I was on a journey that would take me to a better place where I belonged.

CHAPTER THREE

High School Struggles

"Whatever you think you can do,
or believe you can do, begin it.
Action has magic, grace and power in it."
Goethe

At 14 years of age in September 1952, after teaching private lessons to students of Holy Family Elementary School for 3 years, I had earned enough money to pay for one year's tuition at high school. The headmistress, American white Catholic nun Sr. Philomena, took me to American white Catholic priest Father MacMullan, headmaster of St. George's College and requested that he enroll me in the high school. Fr. MacMullan agreed to admit me into First form. Sr. Philomena asked, "In what form are students of his age?"

He answered "Third form, but those students have already been taught subjects such as algebra, geometry and Latin, which Peter has never done."

"I believe Peter will be able to catch up with the other students in those subjects" she declared, "and I want you to try him in third form with students of his own age."

Fr. McMullan conceded, "I will try him in second form, but if he cannot manage I will have to move him down to first form."

Sr. Philomena kept insisting, "I believe he will cope in third form. If he cannot manage, then move him down to second form; and if he still cannot manage, move him again down to first form."

Fr. MacMullan eventually gave in, "OK, I will try him in third form, but I know it cannot work."

My heart swelled with pride at Sr. Philomena's unwavering confidence in my academic ability. I silently vowed to do my very best to justify her faith in me and to prove to Fr. McMullan that I could manage third form studies.

He would have to eat his words as I came third in the first term of form 3A, and first in every term of every form thereafter for all three years before graduation. I did not have the money to buy all of the assigned schoolbooks and had to resort to borrowing similar subject textbooks that I could find from either the school or public libraries. I copied the homework assignments from a classmate's textbook. My first mathematics teacher was Mr. Raftery, an inexperienced young teacher studying to be a priest. Mr. Chaplin, the senior mathematics teacher recognized as one of the best in Jamaica, taught three of the other four third forms. Yet to my surprise, I was awarded the Junior Mathematics Prize as the most outstanding student in all five Third forms. I continued to teach extra lessons at Holy Trinity Elementary School, as I had to continue paying my school fees, which my family could not afford. When I had no lunch money, I would walk home at lunchtime, but sometimes there was little to eat and I had to walk back to school still hungry. In fourth form I started teaching private lessons in mathematics to high school students, including one student in my own class. I also got jobs during the holiday periods as a wrapper of merchandise in downtown Kingston stores.

My sisters also benefited from Sr. Philomena's interest in my family. The year after I entered high school she became headmistress of Alpha Academy High School. She gave tuition free scholarships to my sisters June, Sheila and Fay to attend Alpha Academy, and to Laura to attend Alpha Commercial School in the evenings. June informed me that she hated going to Alpha because she was ashamed of the shabby clothes she often wore and the cheap lunches she carried to school. At lunchtime she would sit facing the corner of a classroom hoping that none of her classmates would notice what she was eating. Mama visited Alpha regularly to check with the teachers on the progress of her daughters and June was mortified by Mama's shabby clothes. However, my worn clothes and inadequate lunches did not particularly bother me at St. George's College. I was content to have anything to eat at lunchtime while being able to pay for my high school education. During discussion of my memoirs in 2008 with my elementary school friend Marie, she stated that some students had complained that

Sr. Philomena helped only the children with fair-skin to enter high school.

In my first term at St. George's College a Sixth form student told me that he was a friend of my brother, Rudy Muir, who had graduated two years ago. He was amazed when I told him that I didn't know of any relative named Rudy.

He exclaimed, "But you are the spitting image of Rudy. You are alike in height and complexion. You must be related to him."

That evening I enquired at home if I was related to a Rudy Muir. I received reluctant acknowledgement that he might be a relative, but got no information about the nature of the relationship or where he lived. I realized then that that there was some mystery regarding my paternal grandfather, as neither he nor anyone else with the surname Muir, apart from my family at home, had ever been mentioned to me. I had never before heard of or met another person with my surname. I eventually met Rudy and other members of his family many years later. To this day I still do not know my true relationship with Rudy's family, despite paying the Registrar of Births and Deaths to search their records and advise me of my family tree. My cousin Jackie and I went together and requested separate reports of our family ancestry. We have followed up the Registrar's office several times and I have still not received any report from them. In 2009 when we returned together to their headquarters in Spanish Town, Jackie was shown his file with very little additional information from what he had provided them. I was told that my file could not be found. They promised to continue searching. They would advise me as soon as my file was found. I have not heard from them again.

In Fourth form I was appointed form monitor for my class, responsible for general discipline and coordination of activities in the classroom. My mathematics teacher was an American Catholic priest, Fr. McClusky who conducted the class like a drill sergeant in the army. Every math problem was given a specific format to be followed exactly as he instructed. Some included unnecessary details in my opinion. I decided to omit the unnecessary steps in my homework assignments and earned the wrath of Fr. McClusky when he demanded, despite my answers being correct, that I include all the details he required. I stubbornly refused to comply. On several occasions I was told to write a homework assignment on the blackboard. Whenever I omitted a detail I considered superfluous, he would declare it incorrect and ask another classmate to correct my 'errors of omission'. No mathematics exam was given during the first term. When we received our term reports Fr. McClusky gave me a C grade, and gave a B grade to the classmate whom I was teaching in private lessons! Nevertheless I came first in form 4A that term. At the end of year examinations I finished and reviewed the arithmetic test more than a half hour before the allotted time had elapsed. No one else had finished the test. Seeing that I had finished working, Fr. McClusky came to stand behind me for a while.

Then he went back to his desk and declared loudly for the entire class to hear, "Muir, your answer to the first problem is wrong."

I glanced through the problem again and decided I could ignore his opinion, as I knew that I had the right answer. After he announced, "Time is up" and collected the exam papers, I turned to the classmate beside me and asked him his answer to the first problem. Fr. McClusky told me to leave the classroom and report to the headmaster's office for talking in class. When the exam papers were marked and returned to us I had received 99% for the exam. Fr. McClusky had changed my correct answer, from 7 cm. to 7.0 cm. and deducted 1%.

I was usually a shy, well-behaved, religious, studious child and my steadfast defiance of a teacher and priest was very much out of character. Perhaps my aberrant behavior was largely due to my experience with my grandmother. She was the supreme authority at home; I resented her disgraceful treatment of my mother. I thought it unfair that only she and my father were always well fed while the rest of the family was often hungry; I rejected her view that our poor, black neighbors were inferior to us, and refused to follow her orders to have no contact with them. Apparently my experience at home had developed in me a lack of respect for, and defiance to, autocratic authority, which I believed Fr. McClusky represented.

St. George's College had a games room next to the headmaster's office, which contained two chess sets among other games. After watching chess being played a few times I asked to be taught the rules of the game. The few chess players were happy to teach me and I was soon playing with them. I even managed to win a game occasionally. About a month after I started playing I found a beginner's chess book in the Junior Library, which consisted of ten rules with one chapter devoted to each rule. I studied the rules, practiced the examples and very soon became the best chess player at school. I taught chess to a few of the brightest students I knew and we all improved with better competition. One day we received a challenge from Kingston College, another all male high school located on North Street, on the opposite side of the street about 100 yards away, to play chess with them on a Saturday morning. We decided to go, and six of us turned up at the appointed time. We were totally surprised when we were escorted to a large hall containing about forty students who were members of their active chess club, and the two teachers who coached them. We thought we had come to play informal games against a few of their chess players. We felt intimidated and feared that we would be soundly beaten.

The meet was organized that we would play two matches each against their twelve best players. After the first six games there was an intermission during which refreshments of sandwiches and sodas were served. I was delighted when I won both my matches and we won the match eight wins to two losses and two drawn. We were a happy group leaving Kingston College expressing our surprise and delight that we were actually good enough to defeat a teacher coached club, especially considering that four of us had been playing chess for less than a year. The following year we were challenged by Jamaica College and also beat them easily. After only these two competitions we considered ourselves schoolboy chess champions, as we never heard of any other high school that played the game.

In Fifth form I was appointed captain of Xavier House. On admission to school all the students were assigned to one of four teams called Houses, which competed for supremacy in several sports and other activities. The House captains wore badges with the names of their Houses, and were responsible to organize all their House activities during the year. House Captain was considered the third most prestigious school appointment after Head boy and Prefect, which were exclusive to Sixth formers. In the first term of Fifth form I remember another incident when I was dismissed from the classroom. Fr. McKenzie, our chemistry teacher, was introducing a new chemistry topic to the class. I asked him several questions about the topic because I was interested and wanted to know more. He apparently did not know enough about the topic to answer my queries adequately and became annoyed. He wrote a mathematical type chemistry problem on the blackboard and told me, "Muir, come up here and let's see if you can do this problem."

Realizing that he had not yet taught us how to do this problem, angry feelings rose to boiling point within me. How could Fr. McKenzie be so unfair! I would not submit meekly to this unjust treatment. I went to the blackboard and studied the problem, determined to try to find a way to solve it.

After a while he said to me, "You are not as smart as you think. Go back to your seat and keep quiet."

I retorted defiantly, "I am ready to try it now" and proceeded to write my solution on the blackboard.

When I was finished, he announced," Muir, your answer is wrong."

I coolly re-examined my solution before asking him, "What is wrong with it?'

"Get out of my classroom" he shouted at me. I took up my books and I left.

Some weeks later we were taught how to do the type of problem he had given me to solve. A few classmates congratulated me for having found the correct solution.

In their final year before graduation Jamaican high school students took in fifth form the British Senior Cambridge examinations marked in England. To gain the certificate a student had to pass a minimum of six subjects including English language and mathematics. Some subject results had to be credits or distinctions in order to attain an overall minimum required standard. After taking these exams, a few students asked me how I felt I had done. I answered that I expected to pass all eight subjects and to receive two distinctions for mathematics and chemistry. I heard afterwards that some students were saying that I was conceited because I stated that I would get distinctions. When the results were released I had received six distinctions, five including English and Mathematics at the highest level 1, one distinction at level 2 and two credits at level 3. I had also attained the number one position for all students in Jamaica based on the six distinctions I received. I was elated at achieving better results than I expected and hurried home to tell my mother the good news. That evening there was no cooked dinner and I was given a few water crackers and sugar-sweetened water for dinner. However, nothing could dim the happiness I felt that day and for many days after.

At the graduation ceremony I was the valedictorian speaker and received prizes for 1st in form 5A, 1st in the Senior Cambridge exams, and the subject prizes for Science, Latin, and History. Although I received the highest distinction grade for Mathematics and English I was not eligible for these prizes since I had not taken Additional Mathematics and English Literature. I was astonished that I won the History prize, not because I did not achieve a distinction grade, but because I didn't do much studying, didn't know history well, and had apparently written much less than everyone else in the exam. I finished writing what little I knew in about half the time permitted. Yet many students were still writing their answers after the announcement to stop writing. The graduation ball was held the following Saturday night in the large pavilion hall at Emmet Park, the sports field of the St. George's College Old Boys Association situated north of the high school.

My friend Marie* and I had not seen much of each other during the past three years while I was attending high school. She attended the nearby all-girl catholic high school, Alpha Academy. I visited her home and invited her to go to the graduation ball with me. She claims that I invited her because she was the only girl I was on speaking terms with, but I was certainly very fond of her. I walked to her home from which her father drove us to Emmet Park. A newly formed band, Byron Lee and the Dragonnaires, consisting of recent St. George's

College graduates, had offered to play the music for free and they sounded surprisingly good. This was the very first public appearance of the band, which was destined to soon become one of the most popular and famous bands in Jamaica and the British West Indies. I really enjoyed myself. Marie* looked very attractive and was pleasant company as usual. The band played popular dance music well. Naturally I was still feeling proud for having done so well in my exams, been awarded so many prizes, and been chosen the valedictorian speaker. I believe that I started to have romantic feelings for Marie* that evening. I was still so shy and sexually repressed, however, that I probably did not kiss her before or after accompanying her back home. She agrees that we didn't kiss and claims that she had not known that I was interested in her romantically.

I graduated from high school at age seventeen and entered the adult world of permanent employment for the first time. I applied to the local government body, the Kingston and St. Andrew Corporation (KSAC), and was offered a clerical position, which I gladly accepted. Although the salary was modest, four British pounds per week, I had become the highest paid member of my street gang.

Scholarship Surprises

I had only been working for a few months when Fr. McMullan sent to my home, at the beginning of the next school year in September 1955, to enquire why I had not returned to school. I went to see him after work the following day to tell him that I had left school and was now working at KSAC. He told me that he wanted me back in school because I had the ability to do well in the Cambridge University Higher Schools examinations and go on to university. I advised him that it had been a great struggle and hardship for me to earn my school fees for the past three years; that I had not been able to buy all the textbooks; that I had to do without lunch on many school days. I insisted that I would not return to school under those conditions. He said that he would see what he could do. I should return to see him on Saturday. On my return Fr. McMullan made the following proposal. I would be awarded a tuition-free scholarship. I would also be employed as receptionist/telephone operator, at the priests' residence situated at the north end of Winchester Park, the school's sports field, from 4.00 pm to 8.00 pm Monday to Friday for one pound per week and served dinner daily. He urged me to accept the offer and not to waste the talent God had given me. I accepted and went back to school. I was appointed a Prefect, whose main duties were to set a good example for, and assist the head boy to maintain discipline among the entire student body.

I enjoyed the receptionist job at Winchester Park. I had a fair amount of free time to do my homework assignments and some studying, and the meals were filling and delicious. Initially I sometimes missed the freedom to do as I wished for a few hours during weekday afternoons, especially playing games with my friends at school or home. However, I was proud that I could perform the receptionist job satisfactorily and felt quite grown up. I grew more confident that I could achieve my goals and make a success of my life. A few days after I started working there I had occasion to go into the dining room when the priests had finished eating and I noticed that a lot of food was still left on the table. Remembering my hungry sisters at home I went into the kitchen soon after and asked if I could take home some of the leftovers for my family. I was generously given all the remaining food in an aluminum foil container and great was the rejoicing at home that evening. Thereafter without asking I would receive parcels of food to take home on a regular basis. With the combined income from the job, private tuition and wrapping in stores during holiday periods, I was now able to buy my textbooks and have adequate lunch money. However, since I was no longer able to participate in the weekday activities of the street gang, a process of gradual withdrawal from the group had commenced.

Still a virgin I was now having stronger sexual urges and noticing girls as sexual beings. I had received no sex education whatever from my parents, however, and the religious teaching I had on the subject from the Catholic Church made me believe that sex outside of marriage was a mortal sin punishable by eternal fire in hell. I can't recall feeling any romantic interest toward any of the neighborhood girls. I had been attracted to some of the girls at Holy Family Elementary school but I was too shy and sexually repressed to approach any of them. However, I thought my friend, Marie*, was attractive and I was gradually getting romantic feelings toward her. I knew I cared for her, wanted to tell her and kiss her but I never did. I even thought that she might care for me more than as an ordinary friend, but she never indicated or told me so.

Even after I returned to Jamaica in 1961 from Harvard University in the U.S.A., I still had 'feelings' for Marie*. However, I never told her how I felt about her until December 2009. Yet in my presence several years before, her mother told Marie's daughter, my goddaughter Karen, that I was very much in love with Marie* back then. When Karen left the room she confided in me that she considered Marie's marriage a disaster! I did not inquire and have not heard anything to substantiate her opinion. Perhaps she had hoped that Marie* and I would get married and was still very disappointed.

During Sixth form I was giving some thought to becoming a Catholic priest. No doubt my close association with the priests on the job and their kindness to me were contributing influences. I joined the student society that met with Fr. Quinlan one evening per week to discuss religious issues. At one session the first topic for discussion was birth control. We were told that sex was for the procreation of children and that all forms of birth control except abstinence were sinful.

At these words I felt a rush of emotion rise in me similar to my reaction to a threat. I was painfully aware that my own mother had too many children whom she could not adequately care for. Yet she had a husband with a steady job in a family-owned home. Adjacent to our home was a tenement yard, with a single outside shower and no kitchen, housing families with children living in a single room. Most families consisted of mother and children with no father living in the home. Many of the children rarely attended and very few finished elementary school. Some of the adults could not read or write. If I was so dissatisfied with my life, I reasoned that many of my neighbors were experiencing even greater hardships and heartache. I also reasoned that their lives would be much better if they practiced birth control and did not have as many children to take care of. With my experiences at home and in my neighborhood, I could not accept this teaching. I spoke out passionately in favor of birth control and told them about the awful consequences of having unplanned, unwanted and/or too many children. Fr. Quinlan expressed concern at the consequences, which he explained was the work of the devil, as was birth control. We should obey the will of God and his Word in the Bible as taught to us in his Holy Catholic Church. When I continued to protest, several students expressed their agreement with Fr. Quinlan and tried to persuade me to accept the teaching of the church, but I remained adamant that birth control was necessary to avoid pain and suffering to poor, innocent children. After the meeting ended, some students continued to exhort me to accept God's will or suffer the loss of my soul.

In my second year of 6th form and final year of high school, I was advised to take the U.S. College Board's entrance and achievement tests and to apply for admission to the U.S.A. colleges of my choice. I knew absolutely nothing about U.S. colleges nor was I acquainted with anyone who did. There was a book in the school library, however, that listed major U.S. colleges and universities which indicated the ones that gave scholarship awards to overseas students. I opened pages at random, wrote down the names and addresses of the first six colleges I saw that awarded foreign student scholarships. I wrote to them applying for a scholarship.

After leaving St. George's College I was employed by J. Wray and Nephew Ltd., manufacturers of Appleton rums and other spirits, as a cashier at a salary of five pounds per week. The results of my scholarship applications to universities would not be known for many weeks. However, I opened a savings account at a bank from my first paycheck and started saving the major portion of my salary towards the cost of my anticipated university education. My first permanent job was a pleasant experience as my co-workers were friendly and my supervisor expressed satisfaction with my performance. I was very surprised that the office was staffed entirely by white and light-skinned persons like myself, so unlike my home neighborhood where the overwhelming majority was dark-skinned.

I was also surprised at the lack of security measures and realized immediately that it would be easy for me to defraud the company of what I considered a fortune in a relatively short period of time. Most customers made their payments in cash, often large sums above a thousand pounds, which I would count before issuing a receipt and stamping PAID on both copies of the invoice. After the goods were delivered the office copies of the invoice, delivery slip and receipt were matched and placed in a filing cabinet in a room that was always kept open. If I retrieved all the paperwork and put the cash in my pocket, no evidence would be left of the transaction. Therefore the loss would not be discovered until stocktaking at the end of the month. Management would know that the goods were missing but would be challenged to determine why they were missing and who was responsible. Not only was I never tempted to actually put this nefarious scheme into practice, I regularly received overpayments from customers which I always returned to them. On one occasion when I was paid several thousand pounds, one of the hundred pound packages bound with elastic bands actually contained eleven packs of ten pounds. I could have put two weeks pay in my pocket with no possibility of detection, but I returned the extra money. The paying customer was obviously a junior employee of the purchasing company, and I knew that he might keep the cash for himself. However, I could not keep it for myself as my conscience was much stronger than my need for the money.

One of my best friends from high school, Perry Mirell*, who knew that I was saving money for the purpose of going to college, visited me at home. He had been accepted for admission to law school in England and needed money urgently for pre-registration fees. His family would provide the full amount at the end of the month but that may be too late for the fees to reach England by mail before the deadline expired. He pleaded with me to lend him some money, which he promised to repay in two weeks. I didn't have the full amount he wanted but I loaned him everything I had saved less the minimum balance required to retain the bank account. I did not see or hear from him again until the date for repayment had passed. When I enquired at his home, I was told that he was no longer living there and had left Jamaica to go to England. I was devastated and have never again been able to trust anyone completely until after they have demonstrated that they are worthy of my trust. I have made many loans to family, friends and acquaintances since, but the amount of the loan is never more than I am willing to lose to the borrower. Regrettably I have not been repaid for loans I made on several more occasions, from very small to very large amounts. However, none of the defaulters has ever, and will ever, receive a second loan from me; I would rather, if I decided to help, give them the money as a gift.

The results of the U.S. College Board Entrance exams placed me in the 97th percentile, the top 3% in the world and first place in Jamaica. Kenyon College in Ohio was the first to write me, advising that I had been selected for their National Scholar award. I was to accept the scholarship by a deadline date. I had not heard from any other college as the deadline approached. I replied to Kenyon College accepting the scholarship, although I doubted that I would be able to find the additional funds required for living and other expenses.. Shortly after I received three additional scholarship offers, the most attractive from

Harvard University. Their scholarship award included total tuition, room and board, plus employment by the school throughout the year. I had never heard of Harvard University before my application and was delighted when the Jesuit priests told me that it was one of the best universities in the U.S.A. and the world! I also received an invitation to attend a scholarship interview from the University of the West Indies in Kingston. I advised them that I would not attend the interview as I had already accepted a scholarship from, and would be attending, Harvard University. Kenyon College sent a letter dated May 8, 1958 welcoming me to their campus and enclosed their 'Certificate of Merit To Peter O. Muir National Scholar'. I felt embarrassed to advise them that I had changed my mind and would be attending Harvard University instead. I also advised J. Wray & Nephew that I had received a scholarship to Harvard University and gave them notice of termination of my employment effective at the end of August. They congratulated me, said that they were sorry to lose me, and requested that I should contact them for employment when I returned from my studies.

When I received my final paycheck, imagine my surprise and delight that they included an additional ten weeks salary as Christmas Bonus to assist me with my college expenses. This was totally unexpected as I had not worked for the full year qualifying period, and the annual bonus was not usually paid until mid December. The following year while at Harvard College, I heard that my 'white' office manager at J. Wray & Nephew was being investigated for defrauding the company of thousands of pounds sterling. I had been correct in my assessment of their security weaknesses. The charges were dropped after his family promised to repay the missing money.

CHAPTER FOUR

A Society Asunder

Intertwined with my life story and the objective of MASTACLASS is the crucial factor of understanding the society that we live in and the products of the society. In order to have the impact and make the change desired, it is imperative that the foundation of the lifestyle, way of thinking and behaviors of the masses is deeply understood. Therein we will find the keys to bridge the gap.

In his 1960s book about life in Jamaica, '*Not by Sun Alone*,' George Mikes, an English journalist and author, has an interesting theory linking slavery with Jamaican attitudes to class, sex and grandmothers in Jamaica, that may aptly explain my grandmother's class prejudice, and my state of sexual repression during my teenage years.

He observed, "Jamaican society consisted of three separate and non-communicating layers. On top you have the whites and the large number of white tourists; underneath, is the coffee-colored middle class, slightly more English than the English; and finally, at the bottom, the overwhelming majority of the people, the black masses, sometimes poor but happy, more often poor and unhappy, but whether happy or unhappy, always poor.

One of the first surprising facts one learns is that to be a descendant of slaves is shameful.

White men behaved like beasts; black men were their victims. Yet, to be white means status; to descend from slaves is shameful. Nowadays, it seems, slavery is deemed to be their shame, not ours. To descend from slave owners covers one, well, not with glory, but at least with prestige. Even a slave society is a human society, so it needs its snobbery; not only among the owners but among the slaves too. The favored bastard children of white slave owners turned against the common mass of black slaves. They regarded themselves as the elite. All the slave owners managed to give to those who aspired to be like them was a measure of the worst kind of European snobbery."

He posed the question, "In what does Jamaican society differs from all other societies I know?" and answers, "In their slave-past and also in their attitude to sex. I want to emphasize that slavery is really the dominant issue because the Jamaican attitude to sex also stems from the traditions of slavery. Humanity has always felt the need for a tremendous guilt complex about sex, partly because it is so enjoyable and partly because it preserves the human race. Earlier Christian fathers were against sex, explaining how bad; how very, very bad sex was. Fortunately, however, few people were concerned with the souls of slaves. More slaves were needed and they were encouraged to breed. Consequently they could develop natural and human ways."

In Jamaica today the masses regard sex as something natural; they are not ashamed of it. They start their sex life early and live it vigorously; but they are not promiscuous. They believe there is nothing at all wrong in sex, but they also believe in stable relationships. Living with a man is one thing; marriage is another. Marriage is taken seriously. As Jamaicans do not like seriousness, comparatively few people marry. The mentality of the Jamaican middle and upper classes, however, is that of our own. The New Testament tells us that 'to be carnally minded is death.' St. Augustine decided, at a ripe old age, that lovemaking was silly and sinful, and advocated abstinence. Sex outside marriage was described as a sin. The Jamaican middle class are as 'virtuous' as we are; 'sin' is publicly condemned and only privately practiced."

Jamaica is still regarded as a predominantly 'Christian' country and the official Christian moral attitude to sex is that intercourse is to be practiced only by husbands and wives within marriage. At Independence in 1962, according to Jamaican law, the legal age of consent for girls only, was set at 14 years old. If prosecuted for statutory rape, males of any age may be fined and/or imprisoned. However, girls of all ages are free to indulge in sex without fear of legal sanction. Naturally, many girls below the age of consent happily enjoy sex with willing boys of all ages. In 1988, the age of consent was raised to 16 years, placing the majority of teenage

boys at risk of breaking the law. How many teenage
boys and young men can for long resist the charms
of adoring teenage girls seeking love and sex? In
fact, many boys do not wait for an invitation, but
take the initiative to earn the consent of
precocious, willing, underage girls. Both the church
and the law are largely ignored by teenagers and
young adults of both sexes and in all classes when
it comes to the matter of engaging in sexual
intercourse.

The 2008 Jamaica Reproductive Health Survey
found that the average age of first sexual
intercourse among females aged 15-19 increased
from 15.2 in 2002 to 15.3 years. This translates to
the fact that the vast majority, much more than
50% of this group were victims of statutory rape.
This also suggests that the majority of Jamaican
males are statutory rapists. Yet there are no
expressions of outrage or even concern, that
hundreds of thousands of Jamaican girls are victims
of statutory rape annually. The sexual
irresponsibility of both slave owners and slaves has
evidently been passed on to the younger
generations. Obviously no one wants to change.

In my teenage years, I accepted the church
and upper classes' public condemnation of sex
before marriage as sin, but had not yet learned
that many of them privately practiced sex, not
only within, but also beside and outside of
marriage. The childhood indoctrination that sex
was somehow dirty, sinful, to be practiced only

for the procreation of children, persisted to influence my attitude and behavior in my sexual relations with women throughout my adult years, including forty years of marriage and beyond. I remained a virgin until twenty one years, and can only remember going on one date during my teenage years, taking my friend Marie* to my high school graduation ball in 1955.

After the death of my wife in 2006, a greater transformation in my attitude to sex began. I had already reasoned that since God made men and women sexual beings to enjoy the practice of sex, then sex must be good for them and pleasing to God. But it was not until 2009, after intercourse with a new partner and her criticism of my sexual knowledge and expertise awakened me to the full possibilities and appreciation of sexuality, its wholesomeness and wide-ranging benefits. I researched sexual practices and relationships on the Internet. In a very short while, a whole new world of sexuality opened up to me. My mind was liberated from the chains of anti-sex indoctrination and lack of sexual knowledge. I began to practice sweet, long-lasting foreplay and oral sex with my partner, which brought mutual joy and fulfillment to both of us.

In 2010 I received a message from Josie* on Facebook suggesting that she had been my teenage friend. She stated that she was living in Canada, married for many years, but was desirous of meeting me again. She planned to come alone to Jamaica and in the meanwhile she would create a new email address through which we could correspond secretly. Subsequent to my reply providing my email at her request, she cancelled her Facebook membership and hoped that no one who knew her had seen her message to me. Josie* visited Jamaica in November and after her return to Canada, I emailed her my unfinished and unedited first three memoirs. In her reply, she commented and I quote:

> "All I have are praises for you. I did not know you were so talented. The love story (which I have finished reading) was very juicy. This alone should make your book a best seller." She went on to say "Incidentally, this is something new for your Love Story (if you like). Remember you had given me an L.P. album entitled "You Sweeten Me" by the Merrymen; I still have that album on which one of the songs went on to say 'My girlfriend promise to give me something...' Well that something was fulfilled 50 years later (laugh)."

I have always felt passionate about, spoken and acted against all forms of prejudice and discrimination, inclusive of racial, color, class, as well as sex discrimination. After decades of adulthood, I added religious discrimination to the list. During my childhood years, all these forms of discrimination were practiced as normal, proper, Christian behavior by the Jamaican upper and middle classes and accepted by the poor, black majority. They had sound reason to believe that discrimination was good Christian behavior since the Bible, written and compiled by men, and proclaimed by Christians to be the inspired Word of God, sanctions it, especially in the Old Testament. In Genesis, the first book of the Bible, we read the following passages: Genesis 2 verses 20, 22 'But for Adam no suitable helper was found. ... Then the Lord made a woman from the rib he had taken out of the man, and he brought her to the man'. Genesis 3 verses16: To the woman he said 'Your desire will be for your husband, and he will rule over you.' Genesis 19 verses 7, 8 (Lot said) 'My friends, I have two daughters who have never slept with a man. Let me bring them out to you and you can do what you like with them'. Genesis 25 verses 5, 6: 'Abraham left everything he owned to Isaac. But while he was still living, he gave gifts to the sons of his concubines and sent them away from his son, Isaac, to the land of the east.'

We are left to assume that the daughters got little or nothing. Throughout Genesis, men and sons are portrayed as important, women and daughters as the property of men. In Leviticus 25 verses1, 44-46, the Lord said to Moses on Mount Sinai, 'Your male and female slaves are to come from the nations around you; from them you may buy slaves. You may also buy some of the temporary residents living among you ... and they will become your property. You can will them to your children as inherited property and can make them slaves for life'. Leviticus 27 verses 1-5, 34 the Lord said to Moses 'If anyone makes a special vow to dedicate persons to the Lord by giving equivalent values, set the value of a male between the ages of twenty and sixty at fifty shekels of silver; and if a female, set her value at thirty shekels. If it is a person between the ages of five and twenty; set the value of a male at twenty shekels and of a female at ten shekels.' These are the commands the Lord gave to Moses on Mount Sinai for the Israelites.'

Needless to say, I cannot accept that every word in the Old Testament is the Word of, or inspired by, God. I aspire to be a follower of Jesus' teaching in the New Testament. I am disappointed, however, that the male Jews who wrote the New Testament did not relate a clear repudiation by Jesus of the discriminatory, unjust and wicked practices related in the Old Testament writings. At a residential Church retreat I attended with my wife, a female attendee was asked to read a passage from the Old Testament that was blatantly discriminatory against women. Instantly, anger boiled up within me that the church would deliberately choose a woman to read, to a group with a large majority of women, a message from the Bible, the 'Word of God,' that women were made inferior and subject to men. I told Beverley that we should organize a protest against this and other like Bible passages being promoted by the Church in the future. Beverley urged me not to do this and cause any trouble. Nevertheless, I spoke with many of the females present and not even one would join me in the protest

From childhood, I would not accept that I was intrinsically better than others who were darker or poorer than me. Nor could I accept that the whites, the upper and middle classes were superior to the poor, black masses and me. I rejected their philosophy and their practices of prejudice, discrimination, inequality and injustice. It followed, therefore, and I became convinced, that I was equal to everyone regardless of their race, wealth, power, position, social status, occupation, and education, or whatever other construct humans devise to use as a means of division. I began to realize that my values were different in many respects from my parents, my community, my religion and the Jamaican society. I felt that persons in authority were not always to be trusted to say and do what was true, ethical, moral and/or just. I was now starting on a journey of independent thinking and individualistic behavior. In my teenage years, I began to speak out and challenge beliefs, doctrines, mores and practices I disagreed with at home, school and church, in my community and in the wider society. I had begun to dare to be different.

From early childhood, I disliked my grandmother for her color and class prejudice, especially since it was directed against my own mother, and defied her edict that her grandchildren should not associate with our poor, darker neighbors. I was angry with Papa for allowing and participating in Gangang's ill-treatment of Mama. I passionately wanted to defend and do something to help my mother, but felt impotent and frustrated that I could not. In adulthood, I sympathized with my girlfriend Beverley, when she expressed her resentment at the preferential treatment she perceived her father gave to his sons over his daughters. She complained that she had to spend longer hours working in his shop. She was sent to an inferior secondary school some distance away in Balaclava while her younger brother was sent to the more prestigious, academically recognized high school closer to her home in Santa Cruz. When I observed the autocratic behavior of her father towards Beverley and his wife Ina, I understood why she told me that she didn't want to get married. I could honestly assure her that I would endeavor to treat her with respect and equality at all times.

Unequal treatment of male and female children was and to some extent still is the norm in Jamaican families. It is thought that boys will be boys. Girls should be taught how to serve and please men, who would provide for them. Boys should not do women's work such as caring for children, cooking and washing. They should be educated to their full potential or taught a trade to enable them to support themselves, their women and their legitimate children in marriage. Education was not important for girls and would probably be a waste of resources, since their chief purpose in life was to 'catch a man' capable of supporting them and their children. In adolescence, boys would be allowed to roam, to have girlfriends, in fact, often encouraged to do so; while girls should stay at home. If a girl was sexually involved with a boy without approval, she might be punished, even beaten; and if she became pregnant, heavens forbid, she would have disgraced the family and might be turned out of the home in extreme cases. The family of the boy who got the girl pregnant, however, would blame the girl for being 'careless' and may even encourage the boy to deny that the child is his. In adulthood, men were favored for employment. A less qualified man would be preferred to a more competent woman. If a woman were employed she would probably be paid less than the man would have earned. Her prospects for promotion would also be limited, since women were not considered to be top managerial material. After all, a woman's role was to serve and assist men, not to rule them.

In my adult years I have consistently resisted accepting and following the status quo. I have boldly spoken out against discrimination, inequality and injustice and consequently incurred the disapproval and/or wrath of family, friends, colleagues, church members and employers. My defiant public display of rebellion against the status quo started in 1966 when my wife Beverley and I began attending the 7:30 am service at the Anglican St. Andrew Parish Church. I was surprised that the majority of the congregation was white or light-brown and very few were black. I was shocked that every male; men and boys, were dressed in suits and ties. So was I. Yet the church had only a few fans, which were totally ineffective in cooling the tropical heat as they were hung from the ceiling high above the pews. I was bathed in sweat when the service ended after 9:00 am. I also noticed that fair-skinned members occupied most of the seats in the front pews. When visitors sat in any of these seats, the regulars would ask the occupier to remove from 'their seat.'

The following Sunday I discarded the jacket; wearing a long sleeve shirt and tie. Beverley asked me to wear a jacket but I refused, stating that I would not wear a jacket to regular church service in the hot tropical summer heat. As I walked up the aisle passing the front pews from the south entrance to the church, many heads with disapproving looks turned to follow me to my seat. Beverley kept pleading with me to wear a suit but eventually gave up trying since I adamantly refused to conform to the dress code of the church.

After attending church jacketless for several weeks, the fair-skinned wife of the highest ranking lay member of the Anglican Diocese of Jamaica accosted me to advise that men attending St. Andrew Parish Church were required to wear a suit in church. I advised her that I would not wear a suit to Sunday morning service while the temperature was as hot as it was now in the summer. I told her that Jesus did not wear, nor request that men should wear expensive suits to church. Furthermore, I did not need or want to follow the Jamaican men's practice of wearing suits to feel and show that I was important and superior to my fellow Jamaicans. Her face reddened with surprise and shock at my unexpected response. She recovered to state angrily that her husband didn't need to wear a suit to feel that he was important. Then she returned to her seat and I proceeded to mine. No one ever spoke to me again about wearing a suit. More than a year later, I began wearing the long-sleeve shirt without the tie. Eventually, many boys and later men stopped wearing suits to the church. The upper class' owning of the choice front seats continued for many more years until the rector, after delivering the sermon, expressed his strong displeasure and opposition to the practice. He declared that "From now on, no member was permitted to ask anyone sitting anywhere in the church to get up from 'their seat.' "

The term 'the good old days,' evokes in me, strong feelings of loathing and condemnation. I hardly ever fail to challenge anyone who refers to the good old days in my hearing. I do not deny that they were very good days for the few upper and middle class elite, but I will shout from the hill tops that they were very bad days for the vast majority of the poor, black, lower class masses. In the 1990s, there was a notable incident that illustrates my opposition to the phrase 'the good old days.' A lay leader of my church conducted an email ministry with the members of the church, and also copied his sermons to the Anglican bishops and selected priests. One of the sermons lauded the 'good old days in the fifties and sixties when the Christian Ethic was so dominant in Jamaica.' I replied to *everyone* that he had emailed, and herein quote excerpts from my reply:

"Dear Lucien, I really appreciate the ministry you have been conducting by email. However, in detailing your factors for the ills of today's society, I believe you have omitted two very important reasons responsible for the chaos and violence in Jamaica today. I have a totally different perspective on those 'good old days.' Unfortunately for my mother, she was darker than my grandmother whose house we lived in, and who treated her as a maid she disapproved of. The vast majority of Jamaican children could not go to a high school no matter how brilliant they were. Many middle and upper level jobs in the private sector were mainly restricted to white and fair Jamaicans.

But I was not to understand the extent of the injustice and prejudice in Jamaica until in the sixties. I became a juror, which was restricted at that time to property owners only. I sat on juries where the prosecution gave little circumstantial evidence that was totally unconvincing of any proof. I was shocked when I was told by the majority of my upstanding Christian jurors that the poor, black, accused man in shabby clothes obviously looked like a criminal. Therefore, if he wasn't guilty of this crime, he may be guilty of other crimes, and this was our opportunity to put him away.

Therefore, Lucien, I believe that the discrimination and injustice of those 'good old days' are two primary reasons for the chaos and violence in our society today. Too much injustice and prejudice still exist, and sadly by some of our Christian sisters and brothers, but thankfully not to the extent of former years."

Surprisingly, neither Lucien nor any of the other recipients replied to my email. No one ever spoke a word to me about it, and I will take their silence to mean consent!

In 2014 I took my housekeeper to her doctor, after she fell and hurt her knee. Seated at his desk was my schoolmate Bob, whom I had not seen since 1957 in our high school classroom, 57 years ago. We had a long chat. Eventually I mentioned that I would soon be publishing the first memoir of my upcoming book, Mastaclass Magic, entitled Pride and Prejudice Prevail. I related to him my experience as a juror, and said to Bob, "When I voted 'not guilty', you cannot believe what the majority of my middle class jurors told me to support their guilty verdict." Before I could tell him, he immediately declared, "They said he looked liked a criminal and this was our chance to put him

102

away!" I was shocked that Bob had spoken the exact words with which I meant to have shocked him! I was surprised that he could and would admit that was this was normal, prevailing injustice practiced by many of the middle and upper classes in those times. We chatted for a long time until the nurse came to remind him that his patients were waiting on him!

I was shockingly reminded of the deep class divisions within the Jamaican society by another experience. One morning at my home at Poinciana Grove, I was standing in my front lawn under our huge ackee tree when I saw a police jeep stop beside a shabbily dressed black man who was walking down Molynes Road. He was ordered into the open back of the jeep and as the jeep drove off, immediately without provocation, two policemen kept punching him with their fists to which he did not retaliate. They were soon out of sight but I was very disturbed at what I had seen. Later that same day I telephoned Radio Jamaica's popular radio talk show program, Public Eye, hosted by a prominent lawyer and related what I had seen. To my surprise and consternation, he asked me if I could prove that the incident happened. He said that he did not believe my story, and that he would not tolerate persons who wanted to use his program to slander the police. Then he terminated the call. I am sure that the police would not have beaten a well-dressed white man in daylight on a main street; I also suspect that he would have reacted differently to such a story. This type of flagrant open display of the worthlessness of, and contempt for a poor black man or woman felt by some white, brown and black persons still occur in Jamaica today. Unfortunately, a few incidents are still being reported, of poor, black, unarmed men and women being cruelly beaten on the streets in front of witnesses. Bones broken and even death have been the fate of some by groups of armed policemen for no better reason than a curse word and the claim that they were resisting arrest. Innocent persons in the ghettos are still being shot to death on suspicion of being a wrongdoer, although the police have no knowledge of their identity. Incredibly, often times no one is held accountable!

More recently in July 2009, I was at a party in West Orange, New Jersey, USA, where I overheard a Jamaican born relative of the hostess speak of Jamaica's 'good old days' and expressed the wish for its return to British government so that its people could once again enjoy discipline and good order. Although I was not a part of the group he was addressing, I interrupted their conversation to challenge his assertions. I declared passionately that the years of British government were very bad days for the majority of the non-white Caribbean people starting with the extinction of the Arawak

Indians, through slavery of the Africans and the oppression of their descendants up to the beginning of partial self-government in 1944. At that time, the majority of poor, black Jamaicans were still experiencing discrimination, extreme poverty, mistreatment, an unjust justice system, a lack of quality education and of good job opportunities. I expressed my opinion that the British residents in Jamaica in that period were the most undisciplined people because of their cruel, unjust and discriminatory treatment of the majority of black Jamaicans. I did not wish a return to those bad old days. He did not make any attempt to rebut my assertions, nor did anyone else in his group. It is ironic, that the hostess later that night, asked him, and he agreed, to drive me to the apartment in Manhattan, New York City, where I was residing for a two-month visit. I had a cordial conversation with him and his wife during the long drive. She complained of a headache and I gave her two acetaminophen tablets that I had with me.

Therefore, when for the first time in my teenage years I read Rudyard Kipling's poem "If," it struck a deep chord of meaning and identity within my 'soul.' It became, and will always be, my favorite poem. I feel that I have been able to 'keep my head when all about me are losing theirs.' I have 'trusted myself when men doubt me but made allowance for their doubting too.' I have been 'lied about and been hated' but will not 'deal in lies or give way to hating.' I have 'walked with kings' (or their equivalent at Harvard University) and 'not lost the common touch.' I believe that I have sometimes been able to 'fill the unforgiving minute with sixty seconds' worth of distance run.' I have loved and been loved deeply and passionately. All my personal hopes and dreams have been fulfilled. I have achieved enough financial success to take care of my own needs plus surplus to help others. I am still reading and taking local and online seminars to gain new knowledge. I am now truly happy, no matter what. I am confident and feel proud that I have evolved from being a son of my father to 'being a Man.'

At the end of this first memoir the reader may be wondering how the author managed to acquire MastaClass status from a childhood of poverty, misery, lack of love and affection, and scarce opportunities for quality education and employment. The good news is that the worst of circumstances are not insurmountable for any child if he or she possesses certain attributes, is willing to experience particular benefits, and chooses to pursue opportunities for learning and growth.

RasTafari: Religion, Rebellion, Ritual and Reggae

There is a certain fringe group in Jamaica called the Rastafari (or Rastas) who profess to worship

Haile Selassie as the returned Messiah. In the 1930s, this Negro movement was established with their chief aim to return to Africa, the land of their forefathers. Earlier, Jamaican national hero Marcus Garvey had led an organization known as the Universal Negro Improvement Association (UNIA). Garvey preached "Look to Africa where a black king shall be crowned. He shall be your redeemer." His prophesy was rapidly followed by the coronation of RasTafari as Emperor Haile Selassie 1 of Ethiopia. Rastas see this as the fulfillment of Garvey's prophesy. The religion takes its name from Haile Selassi's original name. Haile Selassi is regarded by Rastafarians as the Black Messiah, Jah Rastafari, who will free blacks from white oppressors and reunite them with their homeland Africa. The phrase, "Back to Africa" became the foundation of the Rasta movement.

The first branch of Rastafari in Jamaica is believed to have been established by Leonard P. Howell in 1935. Howell preached the divinity of Haile Selassi and proclaimed that all blacks would gain supremacy over the whites. The message of Rasta theology spread and brought hope of repatriation to Africa and freedom for the black race. Having previously divided Jamaicans into two groups, 'Jamaica Up' and 'Jamaica Down,' I will term this third group as 'Jamaica Under.' The Rastas were considered the poorest group in Jamaica living almost entirely in Kingston and

Spanish Town as squatters in indescribably filthy slums on land known as "Back-o-Wall." The majority was illiterate, unemployed, and clothed in rags. Their chief distinguishing feature is their long hair and beard both of which are maintained for religious reasons. Other Rastas are clean-shaven, live in well to do areas, and send their children to school.

In 1953, George Simpson of Oberlin College conducted a study of this group. Professor Simpson's report concentrates on RasTafari doctrine, descriptions of street meetings and worship, paying little attention to the history, organization, or background of the movement. In 1960, another study was published by members of The University College of the West Indies staff. The U.C.W.I. report was more comprehensive and tried to bring the movement up to date since extensive changes have occurred since 1953, principally with respect to the growth of the cult and the increasing state of unrest within it, due chiefly to their persecution by the police who are alarmed by its criminal element. The public has also formed an unfavorable stereotype of the Rasta as shiftless, prone to violence, ganja smoking, bearded, and illiterate. The mere sight of a beard was enough to fill its viewer with feelings of fear and contempt.

In the 1970s, I became interested in the RasTafari, because of my love for a new style of music played by the Rastafarians called Reggae.

The main performer of this genre of music who captured my interest was an artiste called Bob Marley, who grew up in Trench Town, a section of the urban ghetto in the western edge of Kingston. I was especially impressed with the lyrics of his music. I bought his earliest albums and played them constantly. When my friends and business associates visited my home and heard his music playing, they would express their disapproval of the awful 'Rasta music' and question why I was listening to such rubbish. I told them that I did not approve of the Rasta movement but I loved the music. I did not, however, tell them that I also loved the lyrics, which struck a responsive chord in my 'soul.' Bob Marley's songs articulated a rebellion against the status quo, against injustice and prejudice and offered hope for change and a brighter future if we fought for it. They made me realize more clearly that I had similar aspirations from early childhood, which had influenced my feelings, my character and my behavior. For instance, songs such as "Get Up Stand Up" brings to my mind confrontations I have had with friends, colleagues, teachers, pastors, and employers when I boldly spoke up for my convictions and acted in accordance with my principles. On some of these occasions I have suffered adverse consequences. But my resolve to be true to myself and to practice what I believe and preach has never been shaken. I will never give up the fight.

Get Up, Stand Up by Bob Marley (Excerpt)

Get up, stand up: stand up for your rights!
Get up, stand up: don't give up the fight!
Get up, stand up: stand up for your rights!
Get up, stand up: don't give up the fight!

Preacher man, don't tell me,
Heaven is under the earth.
I know you don't know
what life is really worth.
It's not all that glitters is gold;
'Half the story has never been told:
So now you see the light, eh!
Stand up for your rights. Come on!

Nevertheless, as much as I liked and identified with his music and his message, I did not initially admire the man. Unconsciously, I was too steeped in the Jamaican middle class culture from my home and conservative Catholicism from church and school to appreciate any good qualities of a Rastafarian, who lived in the ghetto, fathered children outside of marriage with various women, unlawfully smoked ganja and presumably worshipped Haile Selassie as the Son of God.

Bob Marley's first recordings came at the beginning of the sixties and it wasn't until 1964, as a member of a group called the Wailing Wailers, that Bob first hit the Jamaican charts with the recording of the single Simmer Down, a plea for peace among Kingston's rival gangs. Despite its popularity among the lower classes, however, up to and through the 1970s, reggae music remained unpopular with Jamaica's upper and middle classes and was rarely heard on the radio stations. In 1972, the Wailers signed with Island records and produced the album Catch A Fire, which was beautifully packaged and heavily promoted. Bob Marley's climb to international fame and recognition had begun. The albums Burnin, Natty Dread, and Rastaman Vibration followed. But it was the release of the Exodus album in 1977, that properly established Marley's international superstar status. It remained on the British charts for 56 straight weeks and three singles from the album, Exodus, Waiting in Vain and Jamming, which hit the top 10, were all massive sellers. Nevertheless, it was not until my wife and I made our first trip to Europe in the summer of 1978, that we became aware of the tremendous popularity of Bob Marley and reggae music in England and many other countries of Europe. We were astonished to see his albums prominently displayed in most of the record shops. When we mentioned that we were from Jamaica we were often asked if we knew Bob Marley and told how much they loved his music.

It was around this time also, that I got an appreciation for the power of music and the impact that musicians can have. Jamaica was in serious political upheaval and turmoil with deadly, politically motivated strife on both sides of the divide. Bob Marley returned to Jamaica that same time after an absence of two years. Prominent members of the warring factions on both sides of the political divide were tiring of the warfare that claimed so many of their members' lives and began to discuss the possibility of a truce. I do not know who first proposed a peace concert, whether the first initiative came from gang members, the political parties or from Bob Marley himself. I am certain, however, that as soon the idea began to be considered and accepted, all the factions soon realized and agreed that the best person capable of ensuring the success of the concert would be Bob Marley, the Kingston ghetto's musical champion and hero. Wikipedia states that "Ironically, the idea for the One Love Peace Concert came from two such gangsters from rival political factions, who happened to be locked up in the same jail cell together and who both wanted to alleviate the violence. Claudius 'Claudie' Massop (JLP) and Aston 'Bucky' Marshall (PNP) decided that the best means to bring the country together was to use music as a uniting factor and organize a major concert. Quickly realizing that Bob Marley, living in exile in London, was a critical element upon which their success depended, Massop flew to London after being released from jail to convince Marley to perform at the event. Marley accepted the invitation, and the concert was Marley's first performance in Jamaica since the 'Smile Jamaica' concert held days after he was shot in 1976."

The *One Love* peace concert took place on April 22, 1978 to a packed National Stadium. Marley and the Wailers were joined on stage by Peter Tosh, Dennis Brown, Big Youth and Jacob "Killer" Miller. The concert was a tremendous success from every perspective, the quality of the performances, the good behavior and peace that prevailed throughout. Most important, was the public display of reconciliation, friendship and unity by the two rival political leaders, Prime Minister Michael Manley and Edward Seaga, Leader of the Opposition, culminating in the moment when their hands were joined together and held aloft by Bob Marley on stage. It was an electrifying moment, captured by the world's cameras, a moment of triumph for Bob Marley, and for Jamaica.

Marley's song One Love has achieved worldwide acclaim as a unifying force between people of all nations, races, religious and political persuasions. It was the BBC's choice for song of the millennium. Time magazine chose his album Exodus as the *best* album of the 20th century. The New York Times declared Marley "the most influential artist of the latter half of the 20th century". He, his songs and albums have won several other awards including a Grammy Lifetime Achievement Award.

One Love by Bob Marley (Excerpt)

One Love, One Heart
Let's get together and feel all right
Hear the children crying (One Love)
Hear the children crying (One Heart)
Sayin', "Give thanks and praise to the Lord and I will
*   feel alright"*
Sayin', "Let's get together and feel all right."

One Love! What about the one heart? One Heart!
What about? Let's get together and feel all right
As it was in the beginning (One Love!);
So shall it be in the end (One Heart!),
*   All right!*
Give thanks and praise to the Lord and I will feel all
*   right;*
Let's get together and feel all right.
*   One more thing!*

Due to his fame and fortune, Jamaican society no longer considers Bob Marley as a mere Rasta troublemaker, his songs dangerous rubbish and reggae music awful and unfit for airplay. On the contrary Marley is now acclaimed as a cultural icon that has enhanced Jamaica's image throughout the world. There have even been calls for him to be made a National Hero!

In 1972, another art form also contributed to the popularity of reggae at home and abroad. Perry Henzel produced the film "The Harder They Come," which realistically portrayed life in the ghettos of Kingston by Jamaican actors with such liberal use of reggae music and Jamaican patois language that it required subtitles when it was released abroad. The film constructed a story out of ghetto archetypes and culture: the bad gangster, the trickster hero, the violence, sexuality and political conflict. It demonstrated that dynamic creative energies were emerging from the lower class of urban Jamaican society. Jamaicans from all walks of life flocked the cinemas to see the day-to-day lives of their own people expressed in familiar action, native language and unique local music on the big screen. The reggae was not merely background music; it was integral to the film's structure and highlighted its distinctiveness and creativity. 'The Harder They Come' awakened many Jamaicans to new possibilities of creative expression in their own language arising out of their own local experiences. The film achieved a measure of international success and critical acclaim, and has been shown in many countries throughout the world.

Rastafarians believe that ganja is a sacred herb and smoke the weed in their religious services and on other occasions. They defy the laws decreeing the possession and smoking of ganja as illegal, at the risk of arrest, fines and imprisonment. I have never understood the rationale that makes ganja illegal while at the same time promoting the use of tobacco and alcohol, which are proven to be much more harmful to your health and also adversely affect the lives of a significant proportion of society. I suspect that the moderate use of ganja can help in the treatment of certain illnesses and I support its decriminalization for private use. I have personally never used ganja, even though it has been recommended and offered to me free of cost to make ganja tea as a cure for illness. I have done some limited research on ganja at the University of the West Indies library and have come to the conclusion that the laws against the use of ganja in Jamaica were enacted by the former slave owners, not so much for its possible harmful effects, but more for the fear of, and as a useful tool to control, the freed slaves who were its main users at that time. I consider this law to be a grave injustice to the poor people who are arbitrarily targeted by the police, and a disservice to the entire society, since I believe it helps to turn law-abiding citizens into criminals.

My research revealed that when the plantation owners first proposed that ganja smoking and possession be enacted as a criminal offence, a royal commission appointed by the British Government recommended against its implementation. But even if ganja were harmful, what is the purpose of making the use of ganja a criminal offense? What is this draconian law supposed to achieve, and what does it actually accomplish? The law has not stopped people from growing and using ganja, and never will. It has contributed to the alienation of countless persons and whole communities against the police and the entire legal system. Its greatest accomplishment is probably the creation of numerous criminals by locking up formerly peaceful citizens with hardened criminals in brutal and indescribably squalid conditions that turn many of them against society. Who are these persons that this unjust law has made into criminals by persecuting and prosecuting them for peacefully possessing ganja? The offenders are mostly young, black males in poor urban areas, many of whom have families to support. When they are locked away and given criminal records their families suffer; particularly the children who often grow up as delinquents and misfits, and eventually become criminals. Can someone explain to me what the benefit of this law is, what is it supposed to achieve, and what good it is actually achieving?

The Highholborn Street Influence

My cousin, Jackie Stewart, who shared with me fifteen years of living at 11 Highholborn Street, believes that our experiences there were equivalent to taking a degree course entitled, "How to Achieve Success." He insists that I should try to share with the readers the feelings, thoughts, actions, habits, goals, and the philosophy generated from our childhood experiences, which developed the passion that drove us, despite tremendous hardships and obstacles, to follow our diverse individual paths to achieve lasting happiness, amazing love, and personal success. Although I am severely handicapped by my loss of memory of most of my childhood experiences, I will try to identify the key factors and actions that I believe contributed to my personal success. I believe that, whatever your circumstances, some of these attributes can contribute to your own personal success.

Jackie equates his experiences at 11 Highholborn Street to attendance at a 'University of Life,' which instilled in him these qualities necessary for success; *Commitment, Determination, Discipline,* and *Ambition.* Combined with hard work, smart work and opportunity, you are likely to succeed in any occupation you chose to pursue. I agreed that I had acquired these same attributes, which, in addition to my fair skin and intellectual ability, contributed to my success. Apparently, the majority of both our siblings likewise benefited since they migrated to the United States and all did fairly well.

Laura remained in Jamaica and at sixteen years of age married her adult boyfriend. They eventually divorced after having seven children. She started several small business enterprises, many of which failed until one eventually prospered. Although she didn't finish elementary school, Laura is now a successful businesswoman married a second time to her much younger husband, Percy, a retired executive with one of the largest companies in Jamaica and a subsidiary of a British multinational corporation. She has eleven children, the last two for Percy, and declares that she would have liked to have more. Both Jackie and Laura worked very hard and very smart to achieve their success.

No doubt the characteristics identified by Jackie underpinned the efforts we made to successfully achieve our goals. Jackie also read a lot from early childhood and had a good command of the English language. However, he is convinced that fair skin color was also an important factor in getting the best jobs, achieving promotion and upward social mobility. Although he didn't attend high school or university, he was consistently picked out for promotion from more experienced black applicants for jobs and placed in offices in which there were no dark employees. He gained rapid promotions and once, while the supervisor went on leave, he was put in charge of a large technical department after only eleven months on the job, initially as a trainee. However, he acknowledges that his fair skin color was not the main reason for his success. Rather he prepared himself for rapid promotion by learning as much as possible about the work he was doing, including that of his supervisor or manager. If co-workers were doing overtime work that he had not learnt, he would stay without pay to watch how the job was done and ask questions to gain a thorough understanding of its operation.

He related one story that contributed to his meteoric rise in the company due to his ingenuity and great interest in understanding all facets of the business. Here's his story: Jackie discovered that there were manuals explaining and describing how to operate, and fix the problems of the company's technical tasks in a cupboard, which was locked at the end of the working day and reopened each morning. However, he was not permitted access during the day, nor could he borrow the manuals. Determined to study the manuals, Jackie hid one of the books under his shirt when no one was in the room, took it home, studied and made notes, before returning and replacing it the following morning. After he had studied several manuals, one day, there was a problem to which no one in the department could find a solution. Jackie suggested that a series of actions may be of help. Everyone was astonished that a recently hired junior technician had proposed a solution that seemed to have some merit. Having nothing better left to try they followed his instructions, which solved the problem. Word spread throughout the company that he was a genius. A few weeks later, he was promoted and rapidly rose to the position of Operations Manager, supervising numerous employees at an early age. Jackie insists that he is no genius, but that his story proves that determination, preparation and hard work are a recipe for success in any endeavor. He is firmly convinced that adverse material and economic circumstances are only temporary, not permanent, barriers to success; that your physical location and circumstances do not determine your success or failure. He believes that each of us can raise our mind to a level above, to a better place than our current circumstances, and set goals to achieve our dreams by determination and hard work.

It is evident that Jackie always had this kind of motivation and drive. While I have forgotten most details of my interaction with my Stewart family members at 11 Highholborn Street, except my visits to Palm Beach, I feel that I had a close relationship with him. He is only a year older than me. His family moved away in1952 after Hurricane Charlie and my family moved into the rooms they vacated. Even then, I think Jackie was more of a role model to me than my brother Bobby, who showed very little interest in his studies or any ambition to escape from the neighborhood.

This leads to another important factor for achieving true happiness and personal success, which is having good role models. Choosing the right role models to follow has tremendous benefits, the earlier in life the more beneficial they can be. My first role model was my mother who displayed three characteristics necessary for self-love, self-esteem and personal fulfillment. These were caring for others, a passion for learning, and spirituality. From an early age I observed my mother caring for others. I experienced her passion for education as well as her deep spirituality.

Rather than mere self-satisfaction, she displayed a strong determination to achieve a greater good for all her neighbors.

My second role model was Jesus, son of Mary and Joseph of Nazareth. I learned his life story and ministry in Catholic Sunday school classes and was inspired to try to follow his example and his teaching. I was amazed by his love for mankind, so great that he willingly endured torture and death on the cross for their benefit. I was impressed by his unlimited capacity to forgive, even his betrayers, his torturers and a murderer who repented from his life of crime. In my greatest moments of childhood despair for a little love and care, I sought comfort in thoughts of his special love and caring for little children. Jesus' life of unlimited spirituality, caring for neighbor, non-discrimination, forgiveness and acceptance of death on the cross for the good of all mankind had a profound effect on me. Also contributing as role models were the Stewart and Wiles families, who demonstrated love and care for each other, and me.

Early Childhood Learning made a major contribution to my success. Learning to speak the English language properly from infancy, followed by attending infant school from three years of age, together absolutely contributed to my academic success. Proper English was the only language permitted to be spoken in our home. Papa brought home the *Daily Gleaner* newspaper from work to read every day. We probably developed an unusually early command of speaking, reading, writing and understanding the English language. An abundance of disparate reading material was available and utilized at the Institute of Jamaica Junior Library, located only a few blocks away. Reading played an important role contributing to my teenage happiness and success. Reading allowed me to escape from the harsh realities of my childhood. I learned about people, their cultures and their countries from near and far. I was transported from my dreary existence and enraptured by stories of adventure and romance. It expanded my vocabulary, and my understanding and mastery of the English language. It empowered me to express myself orally and in writing, fluently and confidently. It contributed to the quality of my answers to examination questions at school.

Another important ingredient that contributed to my development was the freedom that I experienced in my childhood. Despite the poverty, deprivation and misery I endured, I somehow felt free in many and various ways: freedom of thought, freedom to dream, freedom to care, freedom of choice, freedom to roam, freedom to learn and freedom from fear. I believe the key factor that led to my exhilarating freedom was freedom from the rod. I am of the firm opinion that the rod spoils and damages the child. Modern research has shown that beating children is harmful to both the child and the parent. Murray Straus, professor emeritus of sociology at the University of New Hampshire, found that spanking slows cognitive development and increases anti-social and criminal behavior. Better methods of correction are explaining why the behavior is wrong and depriving the child of privileges. The care that children receive in the early years of their lives largely determines their adult character and behavior. Their childhood experiences form the foundation for their physical, social, creative, mental and learning abilities, their health and their mind. Beating young children not only hurts them physically, but does greater damage mentally. They are unlikely to have done anything wrong intentionally. The beating creates confusion, fear and resentment in their mind, which may lead to loss of creativity, curiosity and initiative. It also teaches children that violence is acceptable behavior.

I can only recall one not very painful beating from Papa for going to the beach instead of to school. Papa paid scant attention to his children's activities. Mama was too busy trying to make ends meet to pay much attention to her children other than checking on their schoolwork. On the rare occasion that she disciplined, she would sit with us to explain why the offending action was wrong, the harm it could cause, and tell us that she expected better from us. Therefore we developed minds free from fear of physical violence and its consequences of crushing our curiosity, creativity and spontaneity. We could therefore acquire an innate discipline from within rather than an external discipline that locks us into a prison of doubt and fear.

The fact that I was neglected as a child may have turned out to be a blessing in disguise. My brother and I were almost totally without supervision. We could roam far and wide away from home, play games and sports on the streets, collect fruits from the neighbors' yards and trees, or just about anything else we chose to do. My most frequent choice of recreational activity on Saturdays and holidays was to read books at the library, while my brother Bobby would be playing sports and games on Highholborn Street. My cousin Jackie chose to escape to his favorite hideout on the roof of the furniture shop next door with a book to read undisturbed. The girls dutifully stayed within our home, except my younger sister Laura who, unknown to our parents, occasionally explored the city after she left home for school. I believe that these 'independent' activities, together with the sparing of the rod, developed in us more freedom of thought, more creativity, more curiosity, more initiative, more thirst for knowledge, more freedom from fear than children who are closely supervised and beaten regularly for whatever reason adults may arbitrarily decide they deserve.

Perhaps it is no coincidence that Jackie, Laura and I have achieved our dreams and are the most successful members of the children from 11 Highholborn Street. Not to be forgotten is the important role and unfair advantage which our fair skin color would accord us in a prejudiced and unjust society over the majority of poor, black Jamaicans aspiring to achieve their dream of a better life. In my childhood I felt trapped, frustrated, helpless, angry and special, different from everyone else. I expected that nothing new would come into my life from others. To make my life better, something new would have to come into my life from inside me. Somehow, I made the decision that I would depend on myself to make my life better. I decided that I would take charge of my life, and that I would work hard and smart to achieve my dreams. Fortunately for me, during my primary school years, I experienced Spirituality, Close Relationships, Quality Learning, Passion, Purpose, Goals and Accomplishments. Important also, was access to the library nearby which offered opportunities for reading throughout my entire childhood. Books were a source of education, entertainment and inspiration.

In my early years I was highly self-motivated to excel in my education. I had a goal that I was dedicated to work for its achievement to the best of my ability. I am convinced that motivation and dedication to realistic and challenging goals are very important factors in achieving success. My plan worked with the help of unexpected advice and assistance from family members, primary and high school administrators at crucial turning points in my life. My mother's total dedication to the education of every one of her children must have impressed and motivated me from a very early age. Witnessing Mama's courage to defy Gangang and Papa at the cistern to insist that I must never miss a day of school for any reason was the major transformational experience of my life. My sister Norma's insistence in my ability to skip a class at elementary school challenged and motivated me to work hard to justify her confidence in me. Coming first after skipping a year of class tuition certainly helped to build my confidence. Sister Philomena's proposal that I accept the job of teaching younger children after school at age eleven demonstrated how much she believed in my ability and challenged me to justify her faith in me. After three years of teaching without receiving any payment Sister Philomena challenged me to manage third form tuition without the benefit of first and second form high school learning. I accepted the challenge, worked hard and placed first in the Form 3B final examinations. My confidence in my ability soared.

Throughout my adult life I felt confident, safe, comfortable and happy. I felt free to follow my soul, to do what I thought was right, to defy the crowd regardless of the consequences. However, I was still thinking that I was different from others, still feeling restlessness, a yearning to be a better person leading a better life. It was not until after my beloved wife died that I began to realize that I was clinging to irrational childhood beliefs and habits in my subconscious mind that were limiting my relationships, my happiness and my success. I have experienced and am undergoing further transformation and clarity to effect the required changes I need for a better life. I have researched, studied and learned a lot more knowledge about the requirements for good health of brain and body, close relationships, attracting your soul mate and financial success. But lifelong habits and emotions are hard to change. The amazing fact is that all habits can be changed. I feel confident that I can change the habits that are holding me back from being the best that I can be.

Depending on your circumstances, it may be very difficult to change the harmful habits and emotions you have acquired from childhood. Nevertheless, you should consider changing the habits that only affect your life negatively. I urge you to find the courage, motivation, dedication and determination that you will need to start you on your own path to good health, lasting happiness, amazing love and personal success.

It will take a lot of willpower to change patterns of behavior you have developed over many years. For instance, if you are sleeping very late at night, waking up late in the morning and rushing breakfast, you should change because this will stress you from the start of your day. Instead, try to sleep as early as possible and wake up early so that you have enough time to leisurely eat a healthy breakfast. This will also give you time to exercise before you go to school or work. First you must identify the bad habits. You must know that you can change them. Then you must decide to change one at a time. You must accept the hard work you will need to shape your better life, and then get to work.

It was not until during my middle adult years that I began to realize the crucial importance of forming and maintaining close, friendly, mutually beneficial relationships with persons who can assist you in achieving your goals. Having a good relationship with your family, relatives, friends, neighbors, fellow students or co-workers can instantly transform your life for the better.

In 2008, during my visit to her Miami home, my sister June related that she was required to plait her younger sisters' long hair and hated it. She recalled that Marjorie was very critical and constantly found fault with everyone's appearance; that Laura was loud and demanding, bossed Sheila and that Sheila in turn bossed Fay. On a subsequent visit to Fay's home in New York, she told me that she remembers June combing her hair. She feels that she was treated unfairly and neglected by both of her parents to such an extent that she regretted being a member of the family.

Fay's strong disapproval of her family persisted into the 1990s. In later years, Fay and I had a close, cordial relationship. She always agreed to my request to accommodate my wife Beverley and me at her home in the Bronx, New York during our vacation trips to USA. We felt welcome and cared for on every visit. Fay agreed to host us again in 1995. A few days before our departure, she confided to me over the telephone that I was the only one of her siblings she really liked. She considered all her sisters hostile to her and she wanted nothing to do with any of them. I disagreed with her very poor assessment of our sisters and she suddenly became hostile to me. She complained for the first time that, during our previous visit to her home several years ago, Beverley had damaged her carpet and she had to replace it a cost of US$400.00. I retorted that I had no knowledge of such an incident. She accused me of lying. I told her I would ask Beverley about it. Her loud voice rang with angry passion into my ear, "You are not welcome in my house." Then she hung up the phone. When I asked Beverley, she could not remember causing any damage to Fay's carpet. Fortunately, at short notice, Hyacinth Alleyne, a dear friend from Jamaica, accommodated us in her apartment at Coop City in the Bronx. Now married and an American citizen, Hyacinth was many years ago the object of my amorous attention in my drunken state while my wife was driving my car after a New Year's Eve party at the Sheraton Kingston Hotel. A few days after we arrived in New York I went alone to Fay's home and handed her at the door US$400.00 cash to pay for the new carpet. She took the money without a word of thanks and went back inside without inviting me in. We had no further contact during my visit. I consider Fay one of the most caring, compassionate and responsible persons I know. I can only imagine the deep wounds from childhood that flared up to cause her aberrant behavior. We have since reconciled during my subsequent visit to New York in 2009 and are close friends once more.

In my seventies I discarded the 'privilege' of being addressed as "Mr.", "Sir", "Boss" or any other label that would indicate that I thought myself *better* than anybody else or that anyone else should think that I am better than them. One morning in June, 2005 I woke up about 5:00 am and started my day as usual with the stretching exercises that cured, and have prevented a recurrence of my severe lower back medical problems many years ago. I had a drink of fruit juice before going to the nearby Queens High School playfield for my morning exercise walk. During the first lap around the field I approached the school gardener weeding the grass and said to him, "Good morning".

He turned around, looked up at me and replied, "Good morning sir". During my last lap before leaving I stopped beside the gardener and asked him why he called me sir in responding to my good morning greeting. "Just a mark of respect, sir", he answered.

I told him, "I do not believe that you are addressing me as sir only as a mark of respect. I suspect that you feel obligated to call me sir because you may believe that I am better than you in some way. I do not agree with that. Being of fairer skin, having a better education and more money does not necessarily make me a better person than you. I am Peter. What is your name?" "Charles". "Good morning Charles". He replied, "Good morning Peter".

I walked home realizing that this was a transformational occurrence in my life. The gardener and I have been on a first name basis ever since. So have most persons I am associated with both before and after this incident, including acquaintances, employees, the postman, the street cleaner, etceteras. I tell everyone that I prefer not be called Mr. Muir, Mr. Peter or Sir. I am Peter.

Not until recently in 2012 did I fully understand and accept that much of human behavior is controlled by the subconscious mind, which acts according to good and/or bad habits learned from our childhood experiences. I now believe that human beings are primarily acting in ways they perceive to be in their, and their loved ones, best interests. I realized that my grandmother's discriminatory and unjust actions may not have been directed by her conscious brain but by bad habits of thinking and acting learned in childhood. I have been able to forgive Gangang and free myself from the remaining shackles of hate that bound and prevented me from being the best that I can be.

In her best-selling book, "Mind Over Medicine, Scientific Proof That You Can Heal Yourself", Dr. Lissa Rankin explains the enormous power that your subconscious mind has over your thoughts, beliefs, emotions, actions, and habits:

> *"Our parents shape the beliefs that reside in our subconscious minds at a young age, beliefs like "You're weak" or "You're going to wind up fat". Your subconscious mind gets filled with beliefs you download from parents, teachers, and others who influence you early in life, filling your mind with the programs that will run your life unless you learn to reprogram your subconscious mind. Usually by the age of six, these programs are written, and few people ever make efforts to examine and rewrite their subconscious programming. Given that we have little control over how this powerful part of our brain gets programmed when we're children, it's no wonder most people struggle to change limiting and self-sabotaging beliefs that can harm not only our health, but all aspects of our lives.*
> *Even if the conscious mind of your adult self is filled with positive, hopeful thoughts, you operate from the subconscious mind 95 percent of the time.*

These habitual negative beliefs, which kick in anytime we're not focusing our attention on positive thoughts, become the default. They operate when we are sleeping, when we're working, or anytime we're not consciously repeating our positive affirmations.

The power of the subconscious mind explains why positive thinking only gets you so far. How many times have you read self-help books, taken workshops, made New Year's resolutions, and vowed to improve your life, only to realize a year later that your life is no better? Since the conscious mind is only functioning 5 percent of the time, it has little power to overcome the weighty influence of the subconscious mind. To effect lasting changes in belief, you must change your beliefs not just at the level of the conscious mind, but in the subconscious mind."

In March 2014 I responded to a request by my friend David Ludtke to join him at his casa in Boquerón, Puerto Rico. During the visit I attended two of the weekly evening sessions to play games hosted by a Puerto Rican couple. Assembled was a large group consisting of Puerto Ricans and visitors from North and South America, Europe and the Caribbean. It was an unforgettable experience of friendship, camaraderie, goodwill, and fun. I was greeted warmly by everyone and received hugs from the hostess and several other women. Everyone participated in the card game which continued until one winner was declared. A delicious dinner was served and then another game started. There was continuous laughter bursting aloud at the telling of jokes and interesting stories. The games sessions and other wonderful experiences during my stay in Puerto Rico triggered the start of another transformation in my life. My eyes were opened to the possibility of a higher level of love, friendship, happiness, caring, and service in the world than I had thought possible. I pledged to be friendlier, more compassionate and considerate of everyone without compromising my principles. I will try to make everyone I meet feel good about themselves, encourage and help them to improve their lives with the power of positive thinking.

I have also recently come to the realization that good parenting is the most important job of every human being. Children live what they learn and experience, especially from their parents and other care-givers in the early years of their lives. Unfortunately too many children, from the highest to the lowest classes, are being taught the use of physical and mental abuse, prejudice and discrimination based on race, sex, culture, religion and class, and the greed for money, possessions and power. As a result, millions of children from poor disadvantaged families learn that crime and cruelty are the only means of survival in an unjust and uncaring world.

I am convinced that good parenting is the solution to solving the most critical problems of the world. It should involve not only the best practices for the physical and mental development and health of the child, but also the inculcation by word, speech, action, and habits of the philosophy that all people are one family under one God. Therefore we should care for and respect everyone everywhere, every time as our brothers and sisters. There will be differences and disagreements of all kinds due to various cultural beliefs and lifestyles but these should be treated with tolerance, compassion and resolve that we can learn from each other and ultimately achieve consensus on the best way forward for all. Parents should protect, love, care for, be the best friend, the role model for their children to the best of their ability. To be the best parent for their children they must first acquire the knowledge and skills, and then resolve to be the best that they can be for themselves, their children their community, their country and the world. Good parenting is the key to a world of peace, love and happiness for all, where we care for each other as one family under one God. If every parent learned, practiced and taught each child this philosophy of life, what a wonderful world it would be.

In conclusion, taking personal responsibility of every aspect of your life is essential for success and happiness. Some of the most important things you can do to better your life include the following recommendations:

- Control your thoughts, emotions, speech, actions and habits with your conscious brain.
- Keep reading, learning new knowledge every day of your life.
- Count your blessings. Maintain a positive, confident attitude.
- Nurture your relationships with family, friends, neighbors, co-workers and others.
- Eat a healthy, nutritious diet consisting primarily of fresh fruits and vegetables.
- Drink adequate amounts of water and fruit juices with no added sugar.
- Take health supplements, in particular, vitamins, minerals and Omega fish oils.
- Sleep an average of seven hours or more per night.
- Do stretching and aerobic exercises daily.
- Set attainable short-term and long-term goals with time limits for accomplishment.
- Work hard to achieve your goals and dreams. Never give up.
- Make time to have some fun every day.
- Yes, you can transform your life and be happy, with the required knowledge, help and support that you need.

APPENDICES

About the Author

Peter Muir was born October 1937 into a poor family located in the Southside ghetto of downtown Kingston, Jamaica. During the 1950s Jamaica had only a few registered, private high schools capable of accommodating less than 10 % of the high school age population. Ten years after Britain had granted Jamaica partial self-government in 1944, not a single public high school had yet been built. Peter's family was so poor that he occasionally attended school barefoot. To fund his high school education he started working at 11 years, teaching extra lessons to students at Holy Family Elementary School. In 1952 at age 14 he entered St. George's College (High School) in Form 3B, skipping two forms. He placed first for Jamaica in the 1955 British Senior Cambridge Examinations. Major high school appointments were House Captain, Prefect and Valedictorian of his graduating class. In 1958 he won an international scholarship to Harvard University for full tuition, room and board. He worked on campus, cleaning dormitories, serving in dining rooms and in the libraries.

After graduation in 1961 with the Bachelor of Arts degree, majoring in Chemistry, he immediately returned to Jamaica. Varied work experiences include high school Chemistry teacher, chief chemist, new products supervisor, sales manager, marketing manager, restaurant owner, chairman and secretary of Shish Kebab Limited. He was the first member of Sales and Marketing Executives International to be awarded an international scholarship to their Marketing and Sales Management Graduate Program at Syracuse University. In 1964 he fell in love with Beverley Hanson at first sight and married her in 1965. The union produced two children, Susan and David. In 1984, Beverley was diagnosed with multiple sclerosis (MS) and designated medically disabled for more than 20 years of their marriage. He retired before age 50 to concentrate on personal investments and have more time to take care of his wife.

He was inducted into the Rotary Club of Downtown Kingston and served as Director of Community Service, Director of Vocational Service, Director of International Service and for many years as Treasurer. He founded a scholarship program in his Rotary club for poor Downtown Kingston inner-city primary and secondary school students. He served as Chairman of the Scholarship Committee and a Trustee of the Scholarship Foundation until his membership status changed from Active to Honorary Rotarian. Volunteering in Youth Opportunities Unlimited, he mentored and tutored teenage inner-city boys. He also served on the boards of community, school, professional, sports and service organizations.

He was awarded Volunteer of the Year 2006 by the Jamaica International Volunteer Committee in association with the United Nations Volunteer Program in recognition of dedicated commitment to community and nation building through voluntary service. At age 77, Peter continues to learn new ideas and discoveries about the health of body, brain, mind and soul. He is happy and excited about his life and his mission to assist in making the world a better place for all people. By sharing his memoirs, he provides invaluable knowledge and personal experiences that you can use to improve your life. He hopes to inspire you to keep learning and striving for a life of close relationships, romantic love, good health, lasting happiness and personal success.

Preview of the Second Memoir

My second Memoir in the *MastaClass Magic* book series, "Lifelong Learning: Your Sure Path to Good Health and Financial Success", tells the story of the efforts I made to become my Best Self; note that this process still continues. I engaged in a lifelong search for knowledge in schools, books, newspaper, seminars, workshops, and the World Wide Web. This significantly helped me to acquire good health and increasing wealth. Notably, when wanting to become an expert, I conducted independent research on a wide range of topics of interest.

After College I focused on achieving financial security to take care of my wife and children, other members of my family and assisting poor children in downtown Kingston with their high school needs.

More recently my studies have focused on Physiology, the study of the functions of living beings; in particular the nutrition of human beings. Readers will learn essential knowledge and practices necessary to develop and maintain a healthy brain, body and mind which will serve them well in every aspect of their life. (For example, you may be surprised to learn that Alzheimer's is due to the progressive disintegration of the brain caused primarily by consuming for decades too much unhealthy foods and beverages.)

There are tremendous benefits to be gained in the *MastaClass Magic* book series, including the following:
- Improve the health of your body, brain and soul
- Develop and maintain beneficial relationships and friendships
- Attract your soul-mate and share wonderful sexual fulfillment
- Enjoy a wonderful, loving marriage and family life
- Learn best practices for parenting your children
- Achieve your goals, your hopes and your dreams
- Become the best that you can be
- Serve your God in spirit and in truth

Mastaclass Lifestyle Recommendations

Tips for Daily Health of Body, Brain, and Soul
On rising drink a glass of water. Each day drink at least 4 liters of water and sugar-free beverages. Avoid regular drinking of sodas, diet sodas, juices, beverages and any other liquids with added sugar or sugar-substitutes.

Do stretching exercises. Back Health exercises are particularly important. During the day do an additional minimum 30 minutes of mild (e.g. stretching, walking, swimming, dancing) and 15 minutes intense (e.g. running, cycling, playing sports, exercycling, weightlifting) aerobic exercises sometime before you go to bed.

Next sit comfortably and inhale deeply for the count of five. Then exhale forcefully through your mouth. Repeat at least 5 times. Deep breathing will energize you whenever you feel tired later in the day.

Say a meditation aloud. (My choice, which you may alter/change to suit your needs): May I be healthy. May I be happy. May I be loved. May (insert family, friends or names) be healthy. May (insert) be happy. May (insert) be loved. (Repeat for all the names of special persons) May all be healthy. May all be happy. May all be loved. May we all have joy and peace in our lives today, and always.

Eat healthy, alkaline meals at least 3 times per day inclusive of fresh fruits (e.g. watermelons, mangoes, avocados), vegetables (e.g. lettuce, pumpkin, callalloo), roots and tubers (e.g. sweet potatoes, yams, and carrots), and peas and beans. Limit the quantity of acid forming foods (e.g. Beef, white bread, sugar, chocolate, coffee, flour, jams, and liquors).

Take health supplements for daily requirements or deficiencies. (e.g. Omega 3 oil, Minerals, B-complex Multivitamins).

Do not smoke tobacco, ganja or anything else. Avoid near contact with smokers since vapors from the cigarette, spliff or pipe may damage your lungs, your brain, your health and shorten your life.

Count your blessings. There is usually air, food, water, clothes, shelter, family, friends, education, books, sports, games, and as many more blessings as you can recall.

Find something positive in all your experiences, good and bad. Remember that a failure teaches you not to repeat what caused it. Seek a new solution and/or find someone to help you achieve success.

144

Do at least one good deed every day. Some cost you little or no money or time. Just a smile, a compliment, a word of encouragement or sympathy may be enough to make someone happier all day.

Read daily, at least a short newspaper/magazine article or a book page, and to learn something new. Do crosswords and puzzles. Play chess, scrabble, dominoes, bridge and other games that challenge your brain. These activities help to keep your brain healthy and wise, and may also lead to future wealth.

Try to ensure that you get 7 hours sleep on average per day. Lack of sleep suppresses your immune system, which makes you more vulnerable to infections. Adequate sleep makes you less likely to get ill, refreshes your brain's ability to make better informed decisions, and makes you look more attractive.

"Love at first sight": Newspaper Article
Avia Ustanny

Family Ties: February 1992 Gleaner Outlook
Sunday Magazine Valentine Feature Article

He went to pick up his sister from the ballroom
dancing lessons at the Little Theatre and met his
future bride. Peter Muir remembers asking his
sister how he could meet the petite beauty. "It
was love at first sight," he says today.

But, Beverley Hanson was very shy and so Peter
joined the ballroom dancing classes to get closer to
her. "I liked him from the start," she now says. 'He
was bright and I like that.' She did not tell him
that, however.

Beverley's parents were in Santa Cruz, and she
took him to meet her uncle with whom she lived in
Vineyard Town. I think they liked me more than
she did', Peter says. He was invited to dinner many
times. Later, she told him that she was not
interested in marriage.

Their first date was at the Carib Theatre where
they saw Dr. No, the James Bond movie. They
courted through the summer of 1964 and got
married on September 12, 1965 – the length of
time it took Peter to convince blushing Beverley
that he was and would be nothing like her father.

Her father, the couple reveal, ran her home in the country with an iron hand.

Would Peter boss her around too?

Peter says, 'I was always a relatively unpretentious type of person in every way – the opposite of a chauvinist. I think for myself – as for men being superior to women – that did not make any sense to me. I told her I did not need anyone to boss around.'

'He most definitely kept his word', Beverley says. 'In fact, his friends say that I am his boss.' Years later, in the eighteenth year of marriage when she was diagnosed with multiple sclerosis, he found it fairly easy to leave his job as marketing and advertising manager at Esso Standard Oil so that he could spend more time at home and look after her.

Today, he cooks, does the shopping and does whatever cleaning may be necessary, as the disease severely restricts her mobility. But, so well has he looked after her that the debilitating effect of the disease has been retarded. She has retained her sight and speaks clearly. Indeed, life with Peter is a laugh a minute. Ever so often she dissolves into hysterical gurgles at some shared joke. They both smile at the memory of her father, Irving Hanson, who was a shopkeeper and Parish

Councilor so wedded to his job that he refused to come into Kingston. He would not have come to the wedding had it not been held on a Sunday.

Peter Muir says that he knows that he loved Beverley more than she loved him at the time of marriage. However, she is now deeply in love with him, he feels. As usual, Beverley admits to everything he says.

What she was aware of in the very beginning was that Peter was an excellent catch. The brilliant son of a poor mother who believed fervently in education, he started teaching at age 11, collecting one shilling per week per student that was kept by his principal, Sister Philomena of Holy Family Primary, who was determined that he should attend high school.

When he had taken all the Jamaica Local Examinations, she brought him to the headmaster at St. George's, Father McMillan, at age 14, who thenceforth took him under his wings until the day he received a scholarship for Harvard in the United States.

At high school, he could not afford to buy books. 'I would borrow books from the school library which were not the texts but which covered the subject matter. I would copy assignments from other student's books', Peter recalls.

Later, his Harvard scholarship covered all the tuition, room and board. Leaving for the college, he said, 'I had never rode in a motorcar before. I borrowed clothes, borrowed a suitcase and went off'.

Peter returned to Jamaica with a degree in the sciences and was much sought after in private sector as a Harvard graduate. Today, he admits that though he has had running battles with supervisor after supervisor, he has never been fired, nor did he ever find it difficult to pick up a job.

He was a catch indeed. Beverley and an ecstatic Peter were married in 1965 and soon she was off to the College of Arts Sciences and Technology (CAST), now University of Technology, to pursue certification in Catering, Dietetics and Restaurant Management.

The couple purchased the Shish Kebab restaurant when it came up for sale, and Beverley proved to be a passionate and able restaurateur until the day she collapsed with a mysterious disease.

The diagnosis of multiple sclerosis, made by doctors in Miami was not negatively received. Beverley herself was convinced that she would recover, and the family, now including son David and daughter Susan was affected by her optimism.

Beverley told Outlook, 'God has been good to me – fantastic...' She says that her husband has helped her a lot with his unstinting support.

Peter temporarily took over the restaurant business when Beverley fell ill, but soon she asked him to leave it, as she would rather have it sold, that not be involved in its running at all. The restaurant was sold and Peter pursued consultancies until he decided to try direct investment, he says.

He did well, having what has been called the touch of gold. Now he is able to work and still be with his wife whenever he wants. David inherited Peter's business savvy, pursuing his own enterprise until suddenly, at age 23, he decided to go to university – much to his mother's ecstasy.

Beverley remains an education fanatic and is proud of the achievements of both her children.

Susan, now a lecturer at UTECH, pursued a double major in Economics and Philosophy at Swarthmore College and completed her Masters at Drexel in Pennsylvania. Back in Jamaica, she also pursued the Masters in Information Systems at the University of the West Indies. David, the 'late developer', graduated summa cum laude from the City University of New York where he majored in

Philosophy and minored in Communications. He achieved his Masters in Social Work. He is now married with two children.

The couple's 30th wedding anniversary was one to remember, they state, as they indulged in an extended honeymoon on the North coast. Two years later, they also went to Hawaii, a trip that Beverley remembers with excitement. The couple continues to enjoy travelling. They are globetrotters of a sort, having been to Europe, all over the United States, Canada, Mexico and the Caribbean.

Peter admits that he has been unable to leave Beverley behind whenever he travels. Even when Susan was just 2 months old, and he was required to travel on business, they asked a cousin to keep the baby while they went off.

They remain a tight pair. They went to church this morning, holding hands as they usually do. They have always been each other's best friend, in every moment of the 37-year old marriage.

Beverley is a passionate gardener, and Peter spends much of his time in investment activities. He is a Rotarian, who has adroitly avoided the presidency for many years. The couple, otherwise, spend hours just talking to each other.

'Women are lovely to look at, but what am I doing with more than one of them?' Peter asks. He has never believed in playing around and frequently engages in debates with colleagues who cannot believe that he enjoys sitting at home and holding his wife's hands.

He says he has never subscribed to following the crowd, never believed in titles, in ostentation, in big positions. 'I am just interested in being happy and having my wife with me,' he concludes. 'We love each other.

Beverley simply rejoins.

The Epitome of Passion: Tribute to Bev & Peter
Allison McGraham

Preamble: This is a tribute to Bev and Peter. I
know that it may sound as though I am eulogizing
Peter as well. I know Peter is still very much with
us, but it's just very difficult to speak only of Bev,
when it has always been "Bev and Peter."

My mother, Mae Holness Young, was Bev's first
cousin, but from my observation, she became Bev's
and Peter's mother, mentor, confidante, counselor,
and friend. Somehow, of her five children, I was the
one often sent from Havendale Drive across to
Poinciana Grove on errands. It was a long walk, but
I never minded because as a little girl who recently
came from the country, I was exposed to new
delights. Among them were the most wonderful
sundaes and my first taste of being grown up when
Bev and Peter showed enough confidence in me to
have me baby-sit six-week old Susan.

As the years went by, Bev became my fashion
standard, with her beautiful shoes and clothes. She
was also the person I went to with issues of the
heart. She never turned me away.

In the ignorance and militancy of my teenage
years, I often jumped to Bev's defense in
arguments with Peter. I was too young to recognize
or understand the dynamics at work between them

– two very strong individuals, equally argumentative and opinionated and *neither* of them *needed* to be defended. Their love for each other and their passion for life, and everything in it, were merely searching for the best way to put down their roots. There is no doubt that those roots were put firmly down. I won't insult them by pretending that it was a *bed of roses* at all times, but the thorns that presented themselves in the Garden of their marriage were dulled by their ability to seek advice, to be patient and to trust their love. As a young observer, I learned some real life lessons that have served me well.

There were always *events* at Poinciana Grove and later Paddington Terrace, where friends like Derrick and Karlene Smith, Guerney and Pam Beckford, Billy and Eppie Rhoden, Marjorie Lewis, Joan Neita, and Hyacinth White plus many others would gather. These friends have remained a part of Peter and Bev's life throughout the years. Friendships were important and were treated accordingly. One *standout* memory for me was the kindness shown, when Bev and Peter hosted a dinner party for my eighteenth birthday.

Bev's adventurous spirit filled me with admiration; she took on new endeavors with great gusto and enthusiasm. I recall:
- the beautifully decorated wedding cakes

- the efficiently run restaurant, which demanded 5 a.m. trips to Coronation Market to get the freshest and the best produce
- the disciplined approach to the gym, and the tennis and swimming lessons
- the love affair with plants and floral arrangements earning her many first prizes [and Cups from the Jamaica Horticultural Society]
- the love of travel

Bev accomplished so very much, and Peter was definitely the wind beneath her wings, because one thing Bev certainly did very *very* well and that was…. choosing a husband. Despite the fact that Bev went through experiences such as the loss of [part of] a breast, the temporary loss of hair from chemotherapy, among many other things, Peter only saw his perfect beautiful wife.

On behalf of the immediate and extended family, I want to publicly to thank Peter for the unstinting love and care he gave to Bev – *never* complaining. He is the epitome of unconditional love. "Yes Peter, we know you did it because you wanted to, and you will say, 'You don't need to be thanked.' But we want to thank you from the bottom of our hearts, for always *enabling* Bev to live her dreams – you pushed her to greatness. There is no way she could have done all she did without you.

For those of you who were not at Bev's sixtieth birthday celebrations, I have to share with you a most touching event. Peter presented Bev with a cup, not a teacup mind you, but a trophy for first prize to the **Best Wife**. And the engraving on the Cup explained that she earned it for the following:

- **Beauty**
- **Intelligence**
- **Personality**
- **Sensuality**
- **Vivacity**
- **Best Dressed**
- **Most Loved**

This presentation elicited two colors among the guests – the women were green with envy and the men red with rage; as some claimed, Peter was "setting them up." So even though illness knocked Bev over, never keeping her down, she triumphed in many ways. How many wives have received or will receive *in their lifetime* such a trophy?

Remember the fashion standard, looking good meant a lot to Bev – MS or no MS. She knew how to get her own way, and Peter humored her. A few years ago, her ear piercing tore. Of course, Peter would take her to have it repaired. But somehow, I got the call for assistance to arrange the procedure and to take her to have it done. That was duly done. A few months ago, even though she was having real difficulty walking, she was still determined to *look her best.* Peter had bought her several pairs of earrings, but the piercing had torn again, and she couldn't wear them... *But she wanted to wear them*, and as we all know, "whatever Bev wants Bev gets." Hence, there was another trip to another plastic surgeon. It didn't matter that I had to lift her unto the operating table because she was unable to manage. One certainly had to admire her determination, persistence and tenacity.

Bev's dance with MS had to be seen first-hand to be believed; once again, she was a source of inspiration. The illness was her challenge and she confronted it head on. She fought with it, and more recently, she graciously bowed to it. She accepted the things she could not change; she had the courage to change the things she could and God *did* give her the wisdom to know the difference.

Bev utilized all the talents with which she was blessed. She never wasted one. Without either of us realizing it, she had a big impact on my life. Bev had that assurance and that special endurance that took her passionately to her final destination. It was my absolute privilege to have been able to tell her how much I love her and to be with her as she so peacefully allowed herself to be embraced by the Light.

www.ingramcontent.com/pod-product-compliance
Lightning Source LLC
Chambersburg PA
CBHW060926040426
42445CB00011B/812